ISO 9001:2008 Internal Audits Made Easy

Tools, Techniques, and Step-By-Step Guidelines for Successful Internal Audits

Third Edition

Also available from ASQ Quality Press:

ISO 9001:2008 Explained, Third Edition
Charles A. Cianfrani, John E. "Jack" West, and Joseph J. Tsiakals

The Internal Auditing Pocket Guide: Preparing, Performing, Reporting and Follow-up, Second Edition
J.P. Russell

Cracking the Case of ISO 9001:2008 for Manufacturing
John E. (Jack) West and Charles A. Cianfrani

Cracking the Case of ISO 9001:2008 for Service
John E. (Jack) West and Charles A. Cianfrani

ISO Lesson Guide 2008: Pocket Guide to ISO 9001-2008, Third Edition
J.P. Russell and Dennis R. Arter

How to Audit the Process-Based QMS
Dennis R. Arter, John E. (Jack) West, and Charles A. Cianfrani

The ASQ Auditing Handbook, Third Edition
J.P. Russell, editing director

Quality Audits for Improved Performance, Third Edition
Dennis R. Arter

The Quality Toolbox, Second Edition
Nancy R. Tague

Mapping Work Processes, Second Edition
Bjørn Andersen, Tom Fagerhaug, Bjørnar Henriksen, and Lars E. Onsøyen

Lean Kaizen: A Simplified Approach to Process Improvements
George Alukal and Anthony Manos

Root Cause Analysis: Simplified Tools and Techniques, Second Edition
Bjørn Andersen and Tom Fagerhaug

The Certified Manager of Quality/Organizational Excellence Handbook, Third Edition
Russell T. Westcott, editor

To request a complimentary catalog of ASQ Quality Press publications, call 800-248-1946, or visit our Web site at http://www.asq.org/quality-press.

ISO 9001:2008 Internal Audits Made Easy

Tools, Techniques, and
Step-By-Step Guidelines for
Successful Internal Audits

Third Edition

Ann W. Phillips

ASQ Quality Press
Milwaukee, Wisconsin

American Society for Quality, Quality Press, Milwaukee, WI 53203
© 2009 by ASQ
All rights reserved. Published 2009.
Printed in the United States of America.

15   14   13   12   11   10   09   5   4   3   2   1

Library of Congress Cataloging-in-Publication Data

Phillips, Ann W.
ISO 9001:2008 internal audits made easy : tools, techniques and step-by-step
guidelines for successful internal audits / Ann W. Phillips.
      p. cm.
Includes index.
ISBN 978-0-87389-751-8 (pbk., CD-ROM)
1. Quality control--Standards. 2. Auditing, Internal. 3. ISO 9001 Standard. I. Title.

TS156.P475 2008
658.5'62—dc22

2008046801

Publisher: William A. Tony
Acquisitions Editor: Matt T. Meinholz
Project Editor: Paul O'Mara
Production Administrator: Randall Benson

ASQ Mission: The American Society for Quality advances individual,
organizational, and community excellence worldwide through learning, quality
improvement, and knowledge exchange.

Attention Bookstores, Wholesalers, Schools, and Corporations: ASQ Quality
Press books, videotapes, audiotapes, and software are available at quantity
discounts with bulk purchases for business, educational, or instructional use.
For information, please contact ASQ Quality Press at 800-248-1946, or write
to ASQ Quality Press, P.O. Box 3005, Milwaukee, WI 53201-3005.

To place orders or to request a free copy of the ASQ Quality Press Publications
Catalog, including ASQ membership information, call 800-248-1946. Visit our
Web site at www.asq.org or http://www.asq.org/quality-press.

∞ Printed on acid-free paper

Quality Press
600 N. Plankinton Avenue
Milwaukee, Wisconsin 53203
Call toll free 800-248-1946
Fax 414-272-1734
www.asq.org
http://www.asq.org/quality-press
http://standardsgroup.asq.org
E-mail: authors@asq.org

Contents

Preface

Implementing the requirements of ISO 9001 can be a daunting task for many organizations. In an attempt to develop a system that will pass the registration audit, we are tempted to establish processes with the primary purpose of conforming to the requirements of ISO 9001. In doing so, however, it is easy to lose sight of the original intent of the standard—to continually improve the effectiveness of the quality management system implemented at our organization.

This book is intended to help managers, management representatives, internal audit coordinators, and internal auditors implement a practical internal audit process that meets the requirements of ISO 9001:2008 while adding significant, measurable value to the organization's bottom line. The tools, techniques and step-by-step guidelines provided in this book can also be used by those organizations that have a well-established internal audit process but are looking for easy ways to make that process more effective. The tools in the appendices of this book have also been provided on the enclosed CD to facilitate your customizing them to fit the specific needs of your organization.

Perhaps the greatest impediment to a truly effective internal audit process is the notion that internal audits should mimic the external audit. We send our internal auditors to Lead Assessor training to learn how to conduct audits. We then use the external auditors as role models with respect to audit preparation, conducting the audit and reporting the audit. The external auditors are, as a rule, extremely professional and quite capable of achieving their desired result. But we fail to appreciate the significant difference in the purpose of internal vs. external audits and thus fail to achieve the huge benefits that can be derived from the internal audit process.

It is my desire that this book will:

- Enable the reader to create an environment where management and employees fully appreciate the value of internal audits in the continual improvement of their organization and thus contribute to their success.

- Provide specific, easy-to-use tools and methods for audit preparation to enable the auditor to dig deeper into the effectiveness of processes and discover findings that will genuinely contribute to the success of the organization.

- Provide techniques that can be used in conducting the audit to tap into the vast expertise of the auditee and find those opportunities for improvement that will result in a significant return on investment.

- Provide specific methods and tools to report internal audit results in a way that encourages timely, thorough corrective action.

Numerous internal auditors have used the tools and techniques presented in this book to conduct process-based internal audits that are encouraged by the requirements of ISO 9001:2008. When they followed the step-by-step preparation guidelines provided in Chapter 5, most new auditors conducted audits that were equally effective or perhaps even more effective than many audits performed by experienced quality management system professionals. Significant returns on investment have been calculated on audit findings discovered by first-time auditors using the tools, techniques, and methods described in this book!

I hope you will find that using these concepts will indeed make auditing to ISO 9001:2008 both easy and effective. Enjoy your journey!

1

Introduction to Internal Auditing for ISO 9001:2008

INTRODUCTION

In helping numerous companies implement the requirements of ISO 9001 since 1989, I have had the privilege of being a part of internal audit processes in a wide range of organizations and facilities. My clients have ranged from small janitorial businesses to global manufacturing companies; from large government agencies to small carton manufacturers. Many organizations develop internal audit processes that fully meet the requirements of ISO 9001 but achieve little else, while others have learned to use internal audits to achieve great successes in their business resulting in a positive impact on the bottom line.

I have studied both types of audit processes in an attempt to understand the secrets of successful internal auditing. Audit processes that meet the requirements of ISO 9001, but achieve little else, have the following criteria in common:

- Management and employees view the internal audit process simply as a necessity to maintain the required certification.

- The organization establishes the internal audit process solely to ensure that it will pass the external audit.

- The primary purpose of the internal audit process is to conform to the requirements of ISO 9001 or other standard applicable to the organization (ISO/TS 16949, and so on).

- Internal auditors emulate the external auditors in conducting their audits.

As a rule, these organizations have not yet grasped the difference between the internal audit and the external audit and thus have failed to achieve the vast benefits that can be derived from an effectively implemented internal audit process.

Those organizations in which internal auditing is used as a vital and effective tool in improving the business and its bottom line have a very different set of criteria in common. These organizations:

- Understand the value of the internal audit in improving the bottom line of the business

- Have clearly differentiated the purpose of the internal audit from that of the external audit

- Base their audits on the effectiveness of processes in the quality management system and the interaction of those processes versus conformance to the applicable standard

- Provide specific tools to enable the internal auditor to conduct audits that are successful in improving the business and its bottom line

It is the objective of this book to share with management personnel, management representatives, internal audit coordinators, and internal auditors the secrets of successful internal auditing and to provide the specific tools and techniques to make it happen.

PURPOSE OF THE INTERNAL AUDIT

ISO 9000:2005 defines an audit as a "systematic, independent and documented process for obtaining audit evidence and evaluating it objectively to determine the extent to which audit criteria are fulfilled." This is certainly true of any audit—whether it is an internal audit, a supplier audit, or an ISO 9001 registration audit. But the purpose of each type of audit is somewhat unique.

The primary purpose of an ISO 9001 registration audit is to verify that an organization has a quality management system in place that meets the stated requirements of ISO 9001:2008. The registrars are specifically trained not to interject their opinions or recommend solutions to systemic problems. Their job is to carefully compare documentation, records, and activities to the requirements of ISO 9001:2008 and verify conformance with the standard. Though the auditors seek information from the auditee, they primarily work independently to evaluate the level of conformance with the standard. Auditees are wisely encouraged by the organization to simply answer the question that is asked and then quietly wait for the next question. Auditees are not encouraged to volunteer information to the registrar.

The purpose of a supplier audit is to verify that the supplier has systems and processes in place to ensure that the customer's specific requirements can be met. Auditors again evaluate documents, records, and activities to ensure that stated quality management system requirements are met as well as specified product or service requirements. The auditees are again advised not to volunteer any information beyond answering those questions that the auditor specifically asks.

Those organizations that have realized the value of internal auditing have discovered that the internal audit is a different animal than the external audit, and that it should be performed in a different manner. In these organizations, the primary purpose of the audit is to find opportunities for improvement and the secondary purpose is to maintain the ISO 9001 registration. The internal auditor brings only half the knowledge to the table that is required for a successful audit—familiarity with the standard, knowledge of the organization's documentation, and a fresh perspective. The auditee brings the other half of the required knowledge—expertise on the process being audited. The two parties are encouraged to work together to identify those processes that are not functioning at their best so that action can be taken to improve them. Such an approach to internal auditing requires a significant culture change in most organizations. Techniques to achieve that culture change are discussed in Chapter 2.

OBJECTIVES OF THE INTERNAL AUDIT

There are four primary objectives of the internal audit:

- To verify conformance to applicable standards
- To verify conformance to documented procedures
- To verify effectiveness of processes in the system
- To identify opportunities to improve the system

In implementing ISO 9001:1994, many organizations emphasized the first two objectives. Audits focused on verifying whether or not the organization conformed with the requirements of ISO 9001 and whether or not activities within the organization conformed to its own documented procedures and instructions.

As the quality management system matured and nonconformances decreased, some organizations sought to make their internal audits more effective. These organizations have focused more on the third and fourth objectives. Audits still verify conformance with ISO 9001 and with the organization's own documented procedures, but auditors are also trained to evaluate the health of the processes within the system. Employees are encouraged to work with auditors to determine specific opportunities for improvement. Internal auditors have been transformed from police figures to continual improvement facilitators. In doing so, internal audits have generated findings that result in substantial, measurable improvements to the business.

ISO 9001:2008 further encourages this approach to internal auditing. Processes within the quality management system must be identified along with their sequence and interactions (reference 4.1.a/b and 4.2.2.c). Criteria and methods must be determined to ensure that the operation and control of these processes are effective (reference 4.1.c). It would then make sense for the internal audits to focus on the effectiveness of these processes and identify where interactions may be breaking down. The best source of information regarding where processes can be improved is the auditee—the expert on the process. Auditees should be encouraged to share their knowledge during the internal audit and thus play a vital role in the internal audit process.

BENEFITS OF AN EFFECTIVE INTERNAL AUDIT PROCESS

There are numerous benefits of an effective internal audit process. They include the following:

- *Reduced operating costs through better efficiency, increased productivity, better planning, and reduced scrap and rework.* Some organizations have calculated actual return on investment on audit findings that have totaled well into six and seven figures in annual returns. Calculating return on investment for internal audit findings is further discussed in Chapter 2.

- *Improved safety performance.* Though ISO 9001:2008 does not specifically address employee health and safety, the requirements of ISO 9001:2008 and the internal audit process can have a positive impact on safety performance. A good employee training process and well-written operating instructions contribute to an effective occupational health and safety management system. When these have been combined with the accountability that audits provide, many organizations have seen substantial improvements in their safety performance just from implementing an ISO 9001-based system.

- *Improved customer satisfaction.* Of course the ultimate goal of any quality management system is improved customer satisfaction. Improved customer satisfaction often leads to an increased customer base. Higher levels of customer satisfaction also lead to reductions in customer complaints and returned product, both of which are costly to any organization in terms of manpower, freight charges, rework, and scrap.

- *Improved morale.* Many organizations beginning their internal audit process will ask, "How do you put the words 'audit' and 'improved morale' on the same page without laughing out loud?" The answer is easy. When employees are encouraged to contribute to the audit process and see improvements made based on their input, audits serve to empower the workforce instead of belittling them.

Several years ago an organization received a visit from their corporate vice president. During the opening meeting for the visit, the VP announced that the organization was postponing efforts to achieve ISO 9001 registration. There were just too many other priorities at that point to spend resources on ISO implementation. Following his opening meeting, the VP participated in a plant tour. During that tour the operators in the plant talked him out of his decision. When the operators were asked why they felt strongly enough about ISO to challenge a corporate vice president, they responded, "Internal audits are the first thing in the quality junk that have actually made a difference. We are finally seeing things fixed that have needed fixing for a long time. And he wants to get rid of it!"

- *Reduced barriers between departments.* Unfortunately, poorly performed audits actually build barriers between departments rather than reduce them. But well-performed audits give employees a chance to work together who have not had that chance before. When someone from manufacturing audits the purchasing process, for example, there will be more understanding of what is required to receive supplies and materials on time. People rarely write "ASAP" on a purchase requisition after they have audited the purchasing process. When auditors from manufacturing see how the lab calibrates instrumentation, they will be less likely to request repeated retests. When the lab sees what it takes for production to pull a sample correctly, they will be less likely to request repeated re-samples. Auditing increases the level of understanding of other departments throughout the organization.

- *Survival.* The ultimate benefit of any internal audit process is survival. Those organizations that have implemented a formal process for continual improvement are the organizations that are most likely to exist ten years from now. Internal auditing can be a powerful tool in any organization's continual improvement process.

The first step in developing a successful internal audit process is creating an environment where management and employees support the audit process and contribute to its success. Techniques to create that environment are discussed in Chapter 2.

Selecting the right auditors for your internal audit team is the next step. Issues to consider in doing so are discussed in Chapter 3. Defining typical roles and responsibilities in the audit process is discussed in Chapter 4.

Chapter 5 outlines a step-by-step process to prepare for an internal audit. Preparation for the audit is the most important phase in ensuring its success. If auditors know in advance what records they will review, how many they will look at, and what they will be looking for when they pull them, they can go out confident that they will conduct a good audit. Tools are provided in the Appendices and on the enclosed CD to assist the auditors in ensuring their success.

Chapter 6 discusses how to conduct the audit in a way that encourages the auditees' input. It will describe how to lead an effective opening meeting, how to establish the correct environment during the audit, and how to handle difficult auditees.

Chapter 7 describes how to report the audit in a way that encourages timely, effective, and thorough corrective action. Though the auditor is not responsible for the corrective action following an audit, there are four things auditors can do to encourage the auditees to take effective corrective action without undue delay. We will examine these four things in Chapter 7.

And finally in Chapter 8 we will look at how to follow up on audit findings to ensure that the corrective action was both implemented and effective. I hope you enjoy the book and get some valuable ideas to improve your internal audit process.

2

Creating an Environment for Successful Audits

GAINING MANAGEMENT'S SUPPORT FOR THE AUDIT PROCESS

The single most important factor in the success of any quality improvement initiative is management's leadership. To solicit that leadership, we often present a series of presentations showing the tools and processes that would benefit the company. As it relates to auditing, we present a series of audit findings along with a list of those who have closed out their findings and those who have not. But this approach often fails to create the energy and support in the management team that is being sought. Management is paid to ensure the financial success of the organization. Speaking the language of money is critical to gaining the support and participation that is needed to make any quality improvement initiative succeed.

An effective internal audit process for ISO 9001:2008 involves evaluating the overall effectiveness of processes, not simply the organization's conformance to the standard and its own documented procedures. (Reference Chapter 5 for a description of techniques that may be used to audit process effectiveness.) If auditors simply quote references to ISO 9001 during the audits and in the report, employees and management are not likely to make timely, thorough corrections and corrective actions. But through evaluating processes and their interactions, an internal audit can pinpoint improvements that will increase the organization's efficiencies, productivity, and ultimate profitability. These findings may account for only 10 percent to 40 percent of the total number of discrepancies. But when problems have been recorded and corrected, the company should make every effort to quantify successes and communicate them to both employees and management.

The review of audit findings at a typical management review meeting will include a summary of audit findings, the status of corrective and preventive actions, and perhaps an update on those required actions that have slipped past their estimated completion dates. But to achieve the level of commitment that is necessary to ensure success of the audit process, the management representative may add an additional comment where appropriate. "Of the 14 audit findings that were recorded in the second quarter, we have been able to calculate return on investment for 5 of them. The ROI came to an annual savings of $952,675." Such an approach will generate a much higher level of interest.

The best method to cultivate the mindset of seeing return on investment in audit findings is to discuss specific findings in specific companies for which return on investment has been calculated and reported. Many of these findings are quite common and may even look familiar.

FINDING:

"There is no training process for new technical employees who affect product quality—for example, process engineers and lab chemists."

ISO 9001:2008 requires that the organization determine the necessary competence for personnel performing work affecting product quality either directly or indirectly and either provide training or take some other appropriate action to satisfy those needs. (Reference 6.2.2.a and 6.2.2.b in ISO 9001:2008 as well as the note in 6.2.1.) Technical and management personnel often directly impact product quality but are frequently omitted from the training process.

The auditor could cite the finding as stated above and generate little enthusiasm in developing a training process for technical employees. Or the auditor could spend just a few minutes investigating how the lack of such a process had actually impacted the effectiveness of engineering and lab-related processes. When a discrepancy is noted during the audit, the auditor should ask, "Has this caused a problem for you or the organization?" Where no training process exists for technical employees, a discussion with new engineers or chemists could reveal significant errors that were made due to the employee not being familiar with specific product or process validation requirements, regulatory requirements, customer requirements, project management requirements, document control requirements, and so on. In one recent audit, two quality system failures caused by the lack of training were documented at $250,000 for the first event and $1.2 million for the second.

The finding can then be documented as follows:

"There is no training process for technical employees who affect product quality—for example, process engineers and lab chemists. The lack of such a process was identified as a primary cause of two recent quality problems."

At the closing meeting, the auditor should report the lack of identified competence requirements for technical employees and the lack of a process to meet those requirements as a discrepancy against 6.2.2.a and 6.2.2.b of the standard. But the auditor should then go on to state, "The lack of such a system was identified to be a primary cause of two breakdowns that cost the company a total of $1.45 million. If we could get our arms around this issue and prevent a similar occurrence in the future, it would be well worth our effort."

FINDING:

"The Customer Specification Book in the lab is obsolete and not included on the Customer Service distribution list for customer specifications."

There are a number of issues related with this finding. ISO 9001:2008 requires that the organization revise relevant documents when product requirements are changed and that relevant personnel be made aware the changed requirements (reference 7.2.2). ISO 9001:2008 also requires that documents required by the quality management system must be under control (reference 4.2.3).

Asking, "Has this caused a problem?" revealed that two of the previous five returned shipments were caused by obsolete specifications in the Customer Specification Book. In both instances, the corrective action simply involved updating the specific document that was not current. There was no additional effort to determine the cause of the problem and take action to keep it from recurring (reference 8.5.2.b). To have *two* shipments returned for the same reason and not ask, *"Why* were the specs not current?" indicates that the organization does not fully understand the corrective action process. Further study of the corrective action process revealed that to be the case. But for the sake of this discussion, we will simply focus on the two returned shipments.

To understand the cost associated with a returned shipment, first flow chart what happens from the moment the customer calls until the issue has been fully resolved. For each step, determine how much time was spent with handling that step, how much production time was lost (if applicable), and how many actual dollars were spent on the step. Production time may be lost in reworking the product, expediting the production of replacement product, and even during the unscheduled changeover time associated with the expedited order. Actual dollars spent may include freight costs to return the bad product, expedited freight to get the replacement product to the customer, expediting fees to procure raw materials needed to make the replacement product, costs associated with disposing of the returned product, travel expenses for sales or quality personnel who are asked to visit the customer to resolve the issues, and so on.

The finding can then be documented as follows:

"The Customer Specification Book in the lab is obsolete and not included on the Customer Service distribution list for customer specifications. Two of the last five returned shipments met the specs available in the lab, but did not meet the new specs that had been agreed upon by Customer Service."

The cost of the two returned shipments—including freight charges, unloading into dedicated containers, rework of the nonconforming product, and premium freight charges for reshipment—totaled $86,000. Of course the hard costs did not include the damage to reputation and customer satisfaction. Simply updating the Customer Specification Book and asking Customer Service to add this site's laboratory to their distribution list for customer specifications would prevent similar mishaps from occurring in the future.

FINDING:

"Three of the five prints reviewed at the construction site were at least two revisions out of date."

Document control is a requirement of ISO 9001:2008 that is often considered to be a necessary evil needed to achieve registration. But in this engineering and construction firm, problems related to print control proved to be the number one cause of exceptions noted by the customer during the project closure phase, costing the organization in post-completion rework. For many projects, this could account for up to five percent or more of the total project cost. Just a few additional questions uncovered 26 exceptions resulting in rework that were caused by the lack of print control.

The finding can then be documented as follows:

"Three of the five prints reviewed at the construction site were at least two revisions out of date. A total of 26 customer exceptions on a previous project were found to be related to print control problems."

Print control at a construction site is a difficult task. Controlling the interfaces between design engineering, the drafting department, and the construction crew is difficult. But reducing exceptions due to print control by just 20 percent would result in a significant savings for the organization.

FINDING:

"Procedure PR-02 requires that the Production Scheduler forward a production plan to the Purchasing Department two weeks prior to the production run. Purchasing is not receiving the production plan until two to three days prior to each run."

Further questions revealed that the delay in planning information had resulted in numerous late shipments of raw materials. Costs associated with late shipments included:

- 29 lost production hours
- Premium freight charges to expedite the arrival of raw materials

- Premium freight charges for final product to meet the customer's delivery requirements

- Costs associated with unplanned changeovers in production to expedite runs in order to meet the customer's delivery requirements

Asking the auditee, "Where has this caused a problem for the company?" will help generate the categories of lost revenue for your organization.

The finding can then be documented as follows:

"Procedure PR-02 requires that the Manufacturing Scheduler forward a production plan to the Purchasing Department two weeks prior to the production run. Purchasing is not receiving the production plan until two to three days prior to each run. In the past three months, late delivery of raw materials has resulted in 29 hours of lost production time, excess premium freight charges, and costs associated with excess changeovers."

Of course, system breakdowns of this magnitude are rarely the fault of a single employee. Optimizing the planning process in this organization required a cross-functional team of employees who were well trained in root cause analysis and problem-solving techniques. But their efforts resulted in a net return on investment of more than $400,000 annually. Another success for the internal audit process!

In evaluating the return on investment for audit findings, typical sources of savings include:

- Production time

- Reduced scrap/rework

- Productivity improvements

- Premium freight

- Costs associated with customer complaints and returned goods

- Costs associated with design verification and validation failures

- Costs associated with employee turnover

- Costs associated with excess inspection and testing

- Excess inventory costs

- Spare parts for equipment maintenance

Of course, not all internal audit findings will result in such financial benefits. But focusing on the effectiveness of processes in addition to conformance to applicable standards and procedures should result in 10 percent to 40 percent of audit findings that will generate significant return on investment. Quantifying and communicating the successes associated with the internal audit process will generate more support for the audit process.

GAINING EMPLOYEES' SUPPORT
FOR THE AUDIT PROCESS

The people who know best where processes and their interactions are implemented effectively are the people closest to the work. The Maintenance Technician knows better than anyone whether or not the Preventive Maintenance process is effective. The Design Engineer knows better than anyone whether the design process is working effectively and where the opportunities for improvement lie. To effectively audit these processes, the auditor must gain the support of the auditee. The auditee must understand that he or she plays a vital role in the internal audit process.

The best place to start in ensuring that the auditee understands his or her role in the audit process is to provide some basic training. This training is not typically time-consuming and can simply be an agenda item at a regularly scheduled employee meeting, department meeting, or "brown-bag" lunch. The agenda for this training may include:

What is the purpose of an internal audit?

An informal survey of employees in a cross-section of industries has shown that more than 95 percent of employees believe that the internal audit is intended to catch them doing something wrong or otherwise evaluate their job performance. As an opening exercise in my audit classes, I write the word "audit" on a flip chart pad and ask the participants to voice their first thoughts. Printable responses often include:

- IRS
- Fear
- Intimidation
- Someone else coming out here telling me how to do my job
- Pink slip
- Vacation
- Hide and seek
- Clipboard (now this one speaks volumes)

Rarely do employees yell out "continual improvement!" or "the best thing that's ever happened to my organization!"

Many internal auditors believe that the primary purpose of the internal audit is simply to conform to the requirements of ISO 9001:2008. Indeed, ISO 9001:2008 does require that internal audits be performed. But employees and auditors alike need to understand their intended purpose.

As discussed in the previous chapter, the primary purpose of an internal audit is to get better at how we do business. The auditor only brings half of the required knowledge to the table. The auditor should bring to the process an understanding of the applicable standard, knowledge of the documented procedures, and a fresh set of eyes. But in an internal audit, the auditee brings the other half of the knowledge required to perform a successful audit. The auditee brings expertise on the process being audited, how that process actually operates on a day-to-day basis, and where major opportunities for improvement may exist. When participants truly understand what the organization can accomplish through the internal audit process, the auditee will be less likely to run when the auditor enters the department.

Who is the customer of the audit process?

Most employees have never really thought of an internal audit as having a customer. Of course, the textbook answer is that the customer of an internal audit is management. The audit provides management with information necessary to evaluate conformance to the defined quality management system and to identify opportunities for continual improvement.

But, indeed, the auditee is also a customer of the audit. If employees do not have adequate tools, information, training, instructions, or documentation to do their jobs correctly, they may actually benefit from the internal audit and subsequent corrective action. Thus they could be considered "customers" of the audit process. Employees should see themselves as active participants and beneficiaries of the process in order to contribute their much-needed expertise.

How open should employees be during the internal audit?

The answer to this question becomes obvious when the purpose of the internal audit is truly understood. If the organization is indeed using the internal audit process to improve the business, employees should not be afraid of audit findings, but should be encouraged to help the auditor in any way possible to identify potential failures in the system. The auditee provides expertise on the process being audited. To identify breakdowns in the interfaces between processes, it is critical to get the input of the auditee.

Should an organization allow employees to be punished based on audit results? This is a difficult question in some industries, but to prevent the fear that is often associated with the word "audit," most organizations should make it clear that there will be no punitive action based on audit results. See "After the Audit" on the following page for a complete discussion of punitive action following an internal audit.

What will happen with the audit results?

Employees need to understand what will happen with the audit results. Typically, results are reviewed at a closing meeting where management of the area audited will be given a chance to question the findings for understanding and perhaps even begin the corrective action process. A Corrective Action Request (CAR) or your organization's equivalent will be initiated to document the cause of the finding, the action taken to remove the cause, and what was done to ensure that the action taken was effective.

Awareness training should lay a good foundation for employees to understand the intent of the audit process.

The internal auditor can also encourage employees' support for the audit process. The auditor should state that he or she respects the auditee's expertise in the area being audited. The auditees should be invited to bring out any issues that they would like to see addressed in the audit report to ensure that these issues get the attention they deserve. Partnering with the auditee in the audit process will empower the workforce and add more value to audit results.

AFTER THE AUDIT

Should employees be punished based on information that is discovered during an internal audit? This is a difficult question that should be discussed within an organization prior to the first audit. Punitive action can range from a supervisor chastising an employee for allowing a finding to be recorded to terminating an employee based on audit results. When evaluating whether or not punitive action should be allowed—or to what degree it should be allowed—the organization's management should consider the impact that action would have on the quality of future audits.

In a recent audit, an operator confessed that he indeed shipped nonconforming product on a routine basis. In this industry, quality control inspectors are not common. The operators are expected to inspect their own product. Upon further questioning, the operator stated that the company pays him to ship nonconforming product. He said, "My base pay is minimum wage and I have five kids to feed. I get bonus pay for every product that goes on that pallet. I can assure you that if I make it, it goes on the pallet—good or bad."

Of course objective evidence is needed to cite a discrepancy. (See Chapter 7 for more information on audit reporting.) To verify this issue with objective evidence, the auditor visited the shipping department. Seven percent of the product staged to be shipped was found to be nonconforming. Based on this evidence, the auditor wrote a finding that stated, "The incentive system encourages the shipment of nonconforming product."

Upon hearing the finding, the Production Superintendent became quite angry. Slamming his fist on table, he yelled, "I want the operator codes off those products!" The auditor quietly pulled the Production Superintendent aside and explained that the operator was not the problem. The incentive system was the problem. Nonconforming products were not isolated to a single person.

With the correct focus, the organization redesigned the incentive system. Bonus pay for each product was actually increased slightly, but each returned product resulted in the appropriate operator losing 100 points. If the operator shipped only acceptable product, his pay was actually increased by about 4 percent. Customer satisfaction ratings soared and the company calculated a huge return on investment based on eliminating causes of nonconforming product, fewer returned shipments and related costs, and increased business with their largest customers. These successes would not have been possible if the Production Superintendent had been allowed to continue with his original reaction.

In most situations, not allowing punitive action is an easy decision if the organization is trying to minimize the anxiety that is often associated with audits and create an environment of open communication between the auditor and the auditee. But what action should be taken, for example, if the internal auditor discovers falsified records? In most organizations, falsified records are grounds for termination.

Some companies take the stand that there are other processes in place to address personnel performance and disciplinary issues. The internal quality system audit is not the tool to identify these problems. If the organization is depending on an annual quality system audit to identify such issues, it has bigger problems than the individual employee. The supervisory or management system is not effective.

In many cases, falsified records are not unique to an individual. Where audits are conducted at 10:00 a.m. and the auditor discovers production log sheets completed through the end of the shift, this practice will probably be found at more than one workstation. Where this practice has been allowed to continue throughout the organization, the problem runs deeper than employee discipline. In investigating the root cause, the organization's management may consider the following:

- Is there any value to the data? Operators apparently do not appreciate its value. It may be possible that someone became overly enthusiastic about implementing the requirements of ISO 9001 and required documentation of information that is of no value to the organization. This could represent an opportunity to streamline the process.

- Have employees traditionally been held accountable for following procedures and recording data? Depending on the industry, employees may not have been held accountable for following procedures and recording data before ISO 9001. In one audit, employees had consistently recorded the same number on all their log sheets. When asked, operators stated that their supervisors had told them to record the target if the results were within process control limits. The supervisors thought it would look better in customer audits. It doesn't.

- Are adequate resources available to generate required data? In one instance where falsified data were discovered, further investigation found that operators were supposed to sample the product every hour, take the sample to the lab (about a five minute walk), test the sample, and return to the production line to record the results on the production log sheet. If the process was running smoothly, it was possible to do this. But if the operator was needed to resolve process upsets, he or she could not leave the area to perform the required inspection. For years, operators recorded "busy" on the log sheet instead of the test results. When a new production manager threatened jobs if the required testing was not completed, test results were recorded every hour—whether or not the test could actually be run.

- How is this data being used and by whom? In some organizations, data is critical to the effective evaluation of the process. Who is responsible for analyzing this data and what decisions are made based on this information? These issues should be addressed in employee training sessions and supervisors should ensure the accuracy of the data throughout the year.

Where the practice of falsified records is rampant throughout the organization, the auditor should identify the practice so that the root cause can be determined and eliminated.

Where the issues that we have just discussed have been resolved and employees fully understand the consequences of falsified data, some organizations will clearly communicate to employees that punitive action will not be allowed following the audit unless there is a blatant, intentional disregard for established policies—such as falsifying records. This approach is mandatory in certain regulated industries (for example, medical products or aerospace industries). But the rules must be clearly communicated by the organization's management before the first audit so that there is no misunderstanding.

The bottom line is that an organization should clearly establish and communicate the policy relative to punitive action based on audit results. To the extent that punitive action is allowed, fear will prevail during the audit and vital input from the auditee will be lost. Internal audits will lose some of their potential value.

How does a company overcome the fallout resulting from punitive action that followed previous audits when it's trying to create a more open environment in the internal audit process? One practice that has been successful in several organizations is to issue two reports following an audit. The first is issued only to the manager responsible for corrective action and to the management representative, who is typically responsible for tracking the status of corrective actions. This report includes the audit findings and is the traditional audit report that will be evaluated by the registrar.

About 60 days following the audit, however, a second report is issued. This report describes only the successes that have resulted from the last internal audit. It describes those actions that have been taken to improve the quality system, its processes, and the product or service. This report is issued to top management and touts the successes of the audit rather than the failures of the system.

In addition to better communicating the successes of the internal audit process, this approach also encourages timely, thorough corrective action. If the responsible manager knows that what he or she is able to accomplish in that 60-day period will be communicated to the rest of the staff, it encourages a timely, thorough response. Communicating successes resulting from the internal audit process is critical to gaining the support of both management personnel and employees.

3

Selecting and Maintaining the Internal Audit Team

IS YOUR AUDIT POOL ADEQUATELY STAFFED?

There is no perfect number of auditors an organization must have to perform effective internal audits. Some organizations, particularly those in the medical and aerospace industries, are fortunate enough to have full-time internal auditors. Most, however, call upon employees who are already overloaded in their current positions.

The number of auditors you must train will depend on several things:

- The size of your organization

- The type of product or service produced

- How you define the scope of each audit

About the only incorrect answer would be to train a single auditor. Who will audit the internal audit process? Who will audit the other activities performed by the auditor? Unless your organization plans to outsource some or all of the internal audit process, you will need to train at least two auditors.

Other than that, a general rule of thumb is to have enough qualified auditors in your auditor pool to ensure that any one auditor is not called upon to perform more than one audit each quarter. Where internal auditors are asked to squeeze an audit into their already full schedules each month, the audits are often quite shallow and do not result in findings that generate a return on investment.

Many organizations will define an audit schedule that requires one or two processes to be audited each month. (See Chapter 4 for a full discussion on the scope of each audit and the scheduling process.) If you have chosen this schedule and if your organization has a procedure that requires audits to be conducted by two auditors, that would necessitate at least six trained auditors. Where you think you need six, train at least ten. Some employees will love auditing, but others will hate it. With only one exception, I have found that auditors who hate auditing typically do not perform very thorough audits. Let those who do not enjoy it leave the audit team.

WHICH JOB FUNCTIONS SHOULD BE REPRESENTED IN THE AUDIT POOL?

Some audits will require specific expertise in order to be effective. An audit of the quality planning process in the automotive industry, for example, will require some expertise in Failure Mode and Effects Analysis (FMEA), Production Part Approval Process (PPAP), and Advanced Product Quality Planning (APQP) methodologies. An audit of statistical process control (SPC) will require some basic knowledge of the tool. But any employee in the organization may perform most other audits of the quality management system.

The internal audit pool should not be staffed with employees from only the quality department. That approach would encourage the belief that ISO 9001 is a "quality department" standard. In reality, ISO 9001 is more a business management standard that impacts the entire organization. Because of that, auditors should be chosen from throughout the organization.

Selecting auditors from each department, if possible, will create champions of the ISO 9001 system throughout the company. Typically internal auditors appreciate the value of the quality management system and the audit process more than any other employee. With a trained auditor in each department, employees can hear from peers that the audit process is a great chance to initiate action where they know action is needed.

Selecting auditors from each department also provides trained sets of eyes across the organization, eyes that can unofficially watch for system failures throughout the year—not just at audit time.

WHAT PERSONAL ATTRIBUTES MAKE GOOD INTERNAL AUDITORS?

ISO 19011, *Guidelines for management systems auditing*, outlines key personal attributes of an effective auditor. In selecting candidates for the internal auditor pool, the organization should consider those who demonstrate the following attributes:

- *Ethical* – fair, truthful, sincere, honest, and discreet. Auditing involves the investigation of actions taken by fellow employees. The effective internal auditor is one with whom employees feel comfortable talking, someone who can be trusted to handle audit findings appropriately.

- *Open-minded* – willing to consider alternative ideas or points of view. Quite often the auditor will find processes that are implemented in ways that are far different than the processes in their own department. The immediate response is, "This is different than anything I have seen before. It must be a finding." Even registrars struggle with this reaction. In reality, if the process being audited conforms to the standard and the organization's own documentation and if the evidence shows that it is effective, there is no finding. The auditor is not being paid that day to express his or her opinion of the process. The auditor's job is to compare facts and data to the standard, to verify conformance to documented procedures, and to evaluate the effectiveness of that process.

- *Diplomatic* – tactful in dealing with people. Perhaps the greatest attribute of an internal auditor is the ability to treat others with dignity and respect. The auditor must recognize the expertise of the auditee in the daily operation of the process being audited. As findings are uncovered, the auditor must report those findings in a diplomatic manner that respects the expertise of the auditee.

- *Observant* – constantly and actively aware of physical surroundings and activities. The effective auditor must be observant of activities around him and must not focus only on those questions on the checklist. The checklist is a guideline to ensure that basic requirements are covered. It is not meant to be a script for the audit. The internal auditor should follow through on information that is interesting and worth pursuing.

- *Perceptive* – instinctively aware of and able to understand and adapt to changing situations. Often the audit will lead down paths that were not anticipated by the auditor. The effective auditor will pursue those paths wherever they may lead to opportunities for continual improvement.

I would like to add a few more attributes:

- *Persistent and thorough.* It is not the responsibility of the internal auditor to determine the root cause of findings or to calculate the associated return on investment. It may take experts in the process several months to identify the true root cause of some system failures. But if the auditor suspects the cause and can verify that cause in less than an hour, he should pursue the issue to assist in the corrective action process. And to the degree that the auditor can document the impact of the finding on the bottom line of the organization, the Quality Manager and accounting personnel can more accurately calculate ROI.

An example of this trait is illustrated by the auditor who found about 10 percent of incoming component parts being scrapped in production. A quick visit to the receiving department showed that the scrapped parts fully met the requirements on the print. Something wasn't right. A call to engineering verified that the print in Receiving was two revisions out of date. Less than thirty minutes of investigation revealed the cause of the problem to be that the supplier and Receiving had been inadvertently omitted from engineering's distribution list for prints.

- *Curious.* An excellent trait for an internal auditor is curiosity about how processes work—a desire to trace a process from the beginning to the end to verify that interfaces have been well defined and implemented.

If I could summarize the desired personal attributes of an internal auditor, it would be the ability to treat others with dignity and respect. In selecting internal auditors, this personal attribute is more important than the individual's technical knowledge of the processes in the organization. Competencies related to the technical skills of auditing can be provided through training, practice audits, and the provision of appropriate audit tools. Effective audit tools are discussed in Chapter 5. Examples of these tools are provided in the appendices in this book.

HOW CAN AN ORGANIZATION MAINTAIN THE AUDIT POOL?

In talking with some experienced internal auditors, I hear comments such as, "I spend several hours preparing for an audit and get reprimanded by my manager for letting my work slide a little. I then go into an area to conduct the audit and get reprimanded by that manager for finding system failures. Then I report the findings at the closing meeting and get further reprimanded for reporting those findings. Help me understand again why I should enjoy this."

Of course, these issues indicate an organization that must work harder on establishing the right environment for the audit process (see Chapter 2). Beyond that, however, the management representative should make an effort to encourage and maintain the audit team. Specific actions may include:

- Sending the auditor a personal note expressing sincere appreciation for a job well done. In teaching classes across the country, I often ask how many participants have ever received a personal note from someone in their organization expressing appreciation for work they have done. Of the few that raise their hands, I then ask how many still have that note. More than 90 percent of those who have received the note still have it! That illustrates what a small token of appreciation means to the recipient.

- Providing tangible reinforcements that express appreciation for the time spent in the audit process. Organizations often provide a "company dinner" for the auditors and their guests. But we are then asking them to spend yet more hours away from private time with their families. Presenting the auditors with a $25 gift certificate to a nice restaurant of their choice is typically more appreciated. The idea here is to recognize that the auditors may have spent personal time preparing for and reporting the audit and that you are giving them some quality time back with their spouses, families, or significant others.

- Recognizing audit responsibilities in performance evaluations. Auditing provides a significant benefit to the organization and should be recognized in the auditor's performance evaluation.

One of the greatest challenges in performing successful internal audits is finding the time to adequately prepare for and conduct the audit. The preparation process is described in more detail in Chapter 5. It requires studying the standard that is being examined, preparing or reviewing the process model, studying any documentation for the process being audited, and creating a good checklist to ensure that the quality management system is thoroughly covered. Even with the appropriate tools being provided to the auditor, preparing to audit a single process can take several hours. Where can that time be carved from?

If we try to squeeze time into an already full schedule to prepare for an audit, we rarely make it happen. But if we have committed to spend time with someone else, the odds of accomplishing the task increase. The perfect example here is starting an exercise program. If we try to work exercise into our day, time seems to get away before the exercise takes place. But if we commit to meet a friend each morning or at lunch to walk, we typically make the time to be there.

If several processes are being audited in a given month or quarter, plan an audit preparation meeting. The applicable auditors can then meet in a conference room where they can help each other prepare for the audits. Auditors will have a chance to bounce questions off each other to see if they are worded correctly. They can discuss the interpretation of the standard, where it may be in question, or ask questions of other auditors in the room who may be more familiar with the process being audited. If the meeting takes place over the lunch hour, be sure that a lunch is provided.

Selecting the right auditors and maintaining an experienced audit team are important elements in an effective internal audit process.

4

Typical Responsibilities and Authorities in the Audit Process

MANAGEMENT REPRESENTATIVE/ AUDIT COORDINATOR

The management representative, or a delegated audit coordinator, is responsible for administrating and coordinating the audit process. Typical responsibilities associated with this position are described below.

Select the audit team.

ISO 9001:2008 specifies that auditors cannot audit their own work. It further states that the auditors must be selected to ensure the "objectivity and impartiality" of the audit process (reference 8.2.2). The management representative must select auditors who are not directly responsible for the process being audited.

Management representatives often try to walk this line closely. The thinking is, "I'll select Bob to audit the maintenance process. He worked in Maintenance three years ago and knows the department well enough to know where to look for the breakdowns." On the surface, this sounds like excellent reasoning. But in reality, the best internal audits are typically performed by those who know the least about the process. Remember that the auditor brings to the audit his or her knowledge of the standard and knowledge of the organization's documented procedures. It is the auditee who brings expertise on the process being audited. With that in mind, the auditor does not need technical expertise in the processes being audited. Indeed, the more the auditor "knows" about the process being audited, the more he or she is likely to audit on the basis of opinion about that process rather than on the documented requirements.

Many organizations require that two auditors rather than one perform each audit. Again, there is no "correct" audit team size, but there are advantages and disadvantages of each choice. The advantages of auditing in pairs include:

- *It provides a training mechanism for new auditors.* New or inexperienced auditors can partner with experienced auditors to achieve on-the-job training.

- *It provides a second opinion on audit findings.* Many internal auditors do not have enough audit experience to feel completely comfortable making judgments on their own. They often appreciate having a second auditor present who hears and sees the same things and can help make decisions on what should be cited as a nonconformance and what need not be cited.

- *It provides for a note-taker and a question-asker.* Many internal auditors find it difficult to actively listen to the auditee, understand the process, follow-up on interesting issues, and take notes that can be read tomorrow. Using two auditors allows one to record legible notes while the other focuses on the issues being discussed.

But, of course, there are disadvantages associated with using two auditors:

- *Two auditors can be more intimidating than one.* Should the organization want to take advantage of the benefits of auditing in pairs, the intimidation factor can be easily diminished. The note-taker should stand or sit in such a way that the auditee can read the notes as they are being written. This would require that one auditor sit or stand with the auditee while the other faces them to ask the questions. The auditors should invite the auditee to read the notes as they are written. This way, the notes belong to all three participants, not just the two auditors.

- *Two auditors may tend to talk over each other and leave little room for the auditee to contribute to the conversation.* This can be overcome by ensuring that each auditor understands his or her role at any given time. There is one question-asker and one note-taker. These roles can be exchanged throughout the audit in order to give both auditors a chance to participate equally in both roles. When the question-asker reaches the end of his train of thought, he turns to the note-taker and says, "Take it home. Have I missed anything or do you have anything else to add?" At that point the note-taker has the floor. Any questions that have not yet been addressed can be asked at that time.

The decision to use one auditor or two will depend on several things:

- The experience of the auditors

- The type of auditor (full-time or part-time)

- The scope of the audit

- The complexity of the process being audited

A final issue that may come up in selecting auditors is whether or not to use top management personnel as internal auditors. Again, there are advantages and disadvantages. If a top manager wants to spend two days of his or her time to attend internal audit training and another two days to prepare for, conduct, and issue a report for a process audit, the employees will inevitably notice management's commitment to the quality management system. But the presence of a manager during the audit may be quite intimidating to the auditee. If the auditee is shut out of the audit process, you will lose half the knowledge that is required for a successful audit.

Here is a suggestion: If a manager would like to serve as an internal auditor, first hold a small celebration in honor of the fact that you work for a manager who is truly committed to the quality management system. Then ask the manager to partner with an auditor who is not on the management team. The manager should be the note-taker at first and allow the partner to be the question-asker. Auditees who glance at the manager before answering the questions or, even worse, direct their answers to the manager may be seeking the manager's approval. If that happens, managers should remove themselves from the audit team and show their support for the process in other ways.

Determine the scope of the audit.

The most difficult activity in administrating the internal audit is defining the scope of each audit. There are four basic ways to audit an organization:

- *Audit the entire organization at the same time.* This type of audit is performed by the registrar or "corporate" internal auditors. They will audit every process in the quality management system throughout the organization in order to verify that the interfaces between those processes are well defined and effectively implemented.

  This type of internal audit, however, is not typically recommended for organizations with more than 25 employees. For larger organizations, the scope is so large that the sample sizes become very small and there is rarely time to follow up on interesting issues. The audit is also quite difficult to prepare for if the auditors are not extremely knowledgeable of the standard. Each auditor will be expected to read, study, and understand five or six sections of ISO 9001 and five or six process models and the supporting documentation for each process. That can be quite time-consuming.

- *Audit by department or area.* In this type of audit, every applicable process within the area or department is included in the scope of the audit. For example, an audit of the Purchasing Department might include requirements related to:

- The policy statement and supporting objectives

- Control of documents

- Control of records

- Definition of responsibilities and authorities

- Training of purchasing personnel

- The evaluation, selection, and re-evaluation of suppliers

- Placing orders for purchased goods and services

- Handling nonconforming purchased goods

- Supplier corrective action

- *Audit by specific product.* An organization may select a specific product and audit each process that is related to the production of that product. In this type of audit, the auditor may select a specific lot number, batch number, or part number of the final product and audit the processes that related to that product:

  - Handling and storage of the product (if it is still available at the site)

  - Product traceability

  - Final product inspection and testing

  - In-process inspection and testing

  - Control of process parameters while the product was being made

  - Incoming inspection and testing of raw materials or component parts that went into that specific product

  - Supplier qualification for incoming materials that went into that product

  - Employee training for those who dealt with that product

  - Document control of procedures, instructions, specifications, drawings, and so on related to that product

These types of audits were quite common for organizations conforming to ISO 9001:1994, but will be more difficult for those organizations seeking conformance with ISO 9001:2008. ISO 9001:2008 focuses more on the processes and their interactions. To audit each of the processes and verify that the interactions with other processes are effectively implemented requires skills and knowledge that an internal auditor may not have adequate experience to develop.

Audit preparation for these audits can also be difficult for new or inexperienced auditors, because it requires an excellent knowledge of the standard and adequate time to prepare for the audit. Auditing the effectiveness of interfaces between the processes being studied can also be more difficult if the audit is to remain within a single area or department.

In very large organizations or in organizations that are spread out over a large geographical area, these audits will become more practical. But the auditors must be especially conscious of their responsibility to verify that process interfaces involving other departments are effectively implemented. Methods to verify process interfaces are discussed further in Chapter 5.

- *Audit by process in the quality management system.* This type of audit focuses on a single process within the quality management system. An audit of the purchasing process, for example, would include verification that inputs into the purchasing process have been clearly defined, communicated, and implemented and that outputs provide evidence that the process is effectively implemented. In this book, "inputs" will refer to anything needed by those working in the process to ensure that the process is effectively implemented. Inputs into the purchasing process, for example, may include:

  - Well-defined requirements for purchased products (perhaps in the form of raw material specifications, prints, or drawings). These requirements are typically provided by the design function.

  - Timely production or service planning must be able to meet suppliers' specified lead times. These requirements are typically provided by the manufacturing group or service providers.

  - Clearly defined pricing policies provided by management.

  - An effective purchasing software program, if applicable, typically provided and maintained by the IT group.

  - Clearly defined evaluation, selection, and re-evaluation criteria for suppliers. Purchasing, quality, design, and manufacturing personnel often jointly develop these criteria.

  - Well-understood organizational and departmental objectives impacting the purchasing process. Top management typically provides organizational objectives; departmental management then identifies departmental objectives to support the organizational objectives.

To verify the outputs of the purchasing process, the auditor should verify that incoming products are consistently arriving on time and within established specification ranges. An audit of the purchasing process will then require that receiving personnel and users of the purchased products are included in the scope of the audit.

The process audit will also verify that responsibilities and authorities have been clearly defined in the process, that documentation is available to control the process where needed (reference 4.2.1.d in ISO 9001:2008), and that activities conform to requirements of that documentation.

Focusing on a single process allows the auditor to fully verify that the interfaces between that process and other processes have been clearly defined and are effectively implemented. Because most system breakdown occurs between processes, most audit findings that generate good opportunities for business improvement are found when verifying these interfaces. It is for this reason that process audits are the primary focus of this book. Tools and techniques to prepare for and to conduct effective process audits are outlined in Chapters 5 and 6.

The management representative, or designated audit coordinator, should clearly define which processes are to be covered in each audit as well as which areas or departments must be included. Whether the organization audits by area/department or by process, a matrix similar to that provided in Appendix D is an excellent tool to communicate the scope of each audit to the appropriate auditors.

After the entire system has been covered in an initial audit, the organization may choose to provide for more focused attention on those areas that need it. An "X" on the matrix in Appendix D indicates that the specified department or area is critical to the successful implementation of the process and must be audited every time that process is audited. An "O" or an "E" indicates that the specified department or area plays a more peripheral role in the process and can be audited every other year. (The "O" indicates that it is audited during the odd numbered years and the "E" indicates that it is audited during the even numbered years.) ISO 9001:2008 allows for such a schedule when it states in 8.2.2 that audits must be planned based on "the status and importance of an activity." Note that this matrix also ensures that each process is audited each year and that each department or area is audited each year. Though not a specified requirement in ISO 9001:2008, it is good business practice for most organizations and highly encouraged by many registrars.

Establish the schedule, time, and duration of the audit.

The management representative typically schedules the general timeframe for the audit as well as the duration of the audit. Though the specific practices may differ depending upon the organization, most companies develop and issue an annual internal audit schedule in December or

January for the coming year. The schedule typically defines which processes will be audited, when, and by whom.

Receive the report.

The management representative receives the audit report to ensure that the audits are thorough and complete, to log in the corrective action requests, and to verify the status of the system.

Monitor/track corrective action.

The responsibility for monitoring the status of corrective action can reside with any appropriate person or persons in the organization. Some organizations leave the monitoring of corrective action to the manager of the area audited. Though this has proven to be effective in some organizations, it has proven to be ineffective in many others.

In the process audit, many findings can be attributed to a breakdown between two or more areas or departments. Which manager will own the corrective action? Will other managers see the finding as a breakdown in "someone else's" area and not actively participate in its resolution? How thorough will be the corrective action if the responsible party is completely responsible for closing it out? In most effective corrective action processes, there is one coordinator who logs the CAR, tracks its status, follows up with appropriate personnel to verify that action has been completed, and arranges for a re-audit of the finding to ensure that corrective action taken was effective. This process is further discussed in Chapters 7 and 8.

AUDITEE'S MANAGEMENT

The auditee's management plays a critical role in ensuring the success of the internal audit. Management must demonstrate their support of the audit process and their commitment to using the process as a mechanism to improve the business. Specific roles of the auditee's management are described below.

Approve the selection of the auditors.

This can be an emotional issue in discussing audit responsibilities. The bottom line is that the organization must set itself up to succeed in the audit process.

If the manager sees that a former member of the department has been selected to be their internal auditor and the manager knows that the auditor left the department because of personnel issues, the manager has a responsibility to raise the issue to ensure the objectivity of the audit (reference Section 8.2.2 of ISO 9001:2008). In this case the perception of bias is just as important as whether or not bias actually exists.

Certainly the management team has the authority to approve the selection of the external auditor. If the registrar has had previous experience with a competitor, has previously worked with the organization, or has previously treated the organization's employees with a lack of dignity and respect, management has a right to request that the registration company select another auditor. The same right applies to internal auditing.

Inform employees.

To ensure the success of the audit, the auditee's management should notify employees in the department of the upcoming internal audit. The pre-audit meeting with the appropriate personnel might address these issues:

- *What is ISO 9001 and why is it important to this organization?* Why is the organization pursuing or maintaining ISO 9001 registration? Does a major customer require it? Could losing the registration cost the organization a major share of business? If so, employees must be aware of this. If the audit includes regulatory standards (for example, FDA mandated GMP requirements), employees must understand that major nonconformance in a regulatory audit could close the facility. The internal audit must uncover potential nonconformance so that it can be addressed prior to a regulatory audit.

  Is the organization pursuing conformance to ISO 9001 as a mechanism to improve the business? If so, employees must be aware of this. How has ISO 9001 benefited the organization? How has the audit process itself benefited the organization?

- *When will the audit take place?* Though surprise audits may provide a more realistic snapshot of day-to-day operations, nothing will ensure the failure of an internal process-based audit faster than surprising auditees with the audit. Remember that the auditee brings to the table half of the knowledge necessary to ensure the audit's success—his or her expertise in the process being reviewed. The audit process needs the active participation of the expert. That participation will be difficult to obtain if the auditee's day was planned and did not include the audit.

- *What will employees be expected to know?* This is a great time to review the policy statement, its application to the department, the organizational and departmental objectives supporting the policy, how employees impact the organization's ability to meet those objectives, and the current status of the objectives. Employees must also be aware of:

  - Documentation that is available in the department and how to use that documentation

– Activities related to their jobs

"I don't know the answer to that question" is an acceptable answer if the auditee simply does not know the answer to the question.

- *How open should the employees be?* During external audits, employees have been correctly advised to answer the question, answer it honestly, answer it thoroughly, and then be quiet and wait for the next question. Employees must hear one more time that the internal audit is a different activity with a different purpose. Employees should feel free to raise issues to be addressed and use the audit to accomplish its intended purpose—improving the business.

- *What will happen with audit findings?* Who will receive the audit report? Who will be responsible for taking corrective action? How does the corrective action process work?

The odds that managers will adequately cover this information are pretty small without a little help from the management representative. To increase those odds, the management representative should provide a "talk sheet" specifying these questions and answers. The auditor should then verify that the appropriate managers have reviewed this information with their employees prior to the audit.

Provide resources.

As discussed earlier, the customer of the internal audit is the owner of the process being audited. The auditee's management must make every effort to provide the necessary resources to make the audit a success. Necessary resources may include adequate personnel, time to participate in the audit, and access to required records.

Ensure cooperation.

Typically, ensuring that employees truly understand the purpose of an internal audit will encourage employee cooperation.

Provide guides.

Guides may not be required for internal audits. But when internal auditors from sister facilities are used or when the organization is quite large, the auditor may request a guide to help locate records, find the appropriate offices or audit locations, and ensure that safety regulations are followed where required throughout the facility. When a guide is requested, the area or department being audited should make sure that one is provided.

Guides will almost always be required for external auditors. These guides should be knowledgeable of the quality management system and able to locate answers when requested by the auditor. The guide must not answer questions that have been directed to other employees. Guides should assist in the audit process only as requested by the auditor.

Provide facilities.

The auditee typically provides facilities for external audits and not necessarily for internal audits. If facilities are required during an internal audit, the auditors will most often make arrangements themselves. Facilities required by auditors may include a conference room or quiet office, access to a phone, access to a computer and printer, and an on-site lunch.

Determine corrective action.

ISO 9001:2008 clearly states that management of the area audited is responsible for taking corrective action without undue delay. It is neither the auditor's responsibility nor the management representative's responsibility to ensure timely corrective action. The department being audited is much more competent to determine the corrective action that will work best for them.

When an auditor dictates the appropriate action, auditees may demonstrate "malicious compliance." An auditee may do exactly as the auditor prescribes, knowing that negative results will follow. The auditee can then announce that he or she knew the recommendations would fail, but was told to implement them by the auditor. When the auditor dictates the corrective action, the auditor—not the auditee—will own the results. An objective verification of effectiveness of the corrective action will also be difficult if the auditor specified the actions to be taken.

Ensure corrective action is completed in a timely manner.

The management representative is responsible for tracking the corrective action. But it is ultimately the auditee's management that is responsible for timely, thorough corrective action following an audit.

AUDITORS

Of course this entire book describes the responsibilities of internal auditors. The following summarizes their specific responsibilities.

Thoroughly prepare for the audit.

The most important phase of an internal audit is the preparation phase. The methodologies used in preparing for the successful audit are discussed in Chapter 5. If internal auditors know exactly what records they will be looking at, how many they want to pull, and what they will look for, their confidence level increases and the quality of the audit is all but ensured.

The phases of audit preparation include:

- Reviewing the standard. To ensure understanding, the auditor should first review the requirements in ISO 9001:2008 and any other applicable standards relative to the process he or she is auditing. To assist the auditor in understanding the new requirements in ISO 9001:2008, a description of those changes is provided in Appendix E.

- Preparing a process model for the process being audited. Process models will be discussed further in Chapter 5 and sample process models are provided in Appendix A. To construct a process model, the auditor should identify the inputs to that process and the desired or expected outputs. Topics for the audit will include:
  - Have inputs been clearly defined?
  - Are employees getting the inputs they need to ensure that desired results are achieved?
  - Are responsibilities and authorities clearly defined and understood?
  - Has the process been clearly established and documented where necessary?
  - Is the process carried out in accordance with the documentation?
  - Is the process effective in providing desired or expected results?

- Reviewing available documentation. The auditor should then obtain any available documentation and review it for understanding. The documentation should be compared to the standard to ensure that all requirements have been addressed.

- Reviewing previous audit results for trends or other indicators of activities that need special attention.

- Developing a checklist to make certain that the audit verifies the degree to which activities conform to the documented quality management system and the effectiveness of the process in achieving the desired results.

Conduct an opening meeting to initiate the audit.

The purpose of the opening meeting is to establish the environment for the audit and ensure that auditors and auditees are on the same page relative to the audit objectives, agenda, and methodologies. The "group opening meeting" is typically held at the beginning of the audit with as many participants as possible. But the most important opening meeting in the internal audit is that held with each individual auditee. These options are described in more detail in Chapter 6.

Gather data to verify conformance to the documented system and the effectiveness of that system.

Of course, this is the essence of an internal audit. The auditor should partner with the auditee to evaluate the process and look for opportunities for continual improvement. Tools and techniques for conducting the audit are discussed further in Chapter 6.

Report nonconformities.

Nonconformities should be reported right away to give the auditee an opportunity to talk about them. The auditor should take care to avoid emotional terminology that will shut down the auditee. The auditor could simply state, "ISO 9001 requires that we use traceable standards to check the calibration of instruments. Since we don't have those, let me record that so we can take care of it before the registrar gets here." That gives the auditee a chance to say, "Oh, I'm sorry. I must have misunderstood your question. The maintenance department keeps those for us. Talk to Bob and see if he doesn't have what you are looking for."

Many auditors have reported invalid findings due to miscommunication. Talking about the finding in clear terms before the end of the conversation provides the opportunity to clear up any miscommunication before the report is issued.

It is also critical that there be no surprises at the closing meeting. To maintain the credibility of the internal audit process, the auditee should know what issues may be brought up in the report before the auditor leaves his or her work area.

Practice appropriate ethics.

Internal auditors should ensure complete confidentiality with each department they audit. Using an audit experience in one department as a joke in the next department destroys confidence in the audit process.

Avoid corrective advice.

The major pitfalls associated with the auditor prescribing corrective action were discussed earlier in this chapter. But in addition to causing the auditor to own the problem, recommending corrective advice can shut down the auditee.

As mentioned earlier, when I ask audit class participants to yell out their first thoughts when I say the word "audit," many participants have responded with, "Someone else telling me how to do my job." Many employees resent the audit process because they perceive the auditors acting as though they know more about the process being audited than the auditee does. I have heard numerous employees state, "Who does Bob think he is, coming out here telling me how I should do my job? He has never seen this department and I have been doing this job for 20 years." Recommending resolutions to audit findings can be misinterpreted by the auditee.

When an auditee asks the internal auditor for recommendations, however, most auditors feel obliged to provide answers. In an internal audit, it may be appropriate to say, "The lab has a pretty good process for controlling their external documents (for example, ASTM procedures). You might want to take a look at their process." Or, "Do you think it would work if you kept your OEM manuals in one place so that folks would know where to find them when they need them?" In either example, the auditor is making it clear that the auditee is the one who must find a way to ensure that external documents are adequately controlled.

Be able to answer questions.

Perhaps the most common question asked during an internal audit is, "What is ISO 9001 and why are we doing this?" This information should have been covered in an awareness session before the audit, but the auditor must still be ready to answer this question. Other common questions include:

- Will my name be in the audit report?
- What will happen with the findings?
- When will the registrar be here?
- Must I fill out this form for ISO 9001?

The auditor should be familiar enough with the internal audit process, the corrective action process, and the ISO 9001 implementation status to be able to answer these questions for the auditees.

Remain within the scope of the audit.

In Chapter 6, we will discuss the proper use of a checklist. The checklist is not intended to be a script that the auditor reads from. Rather, it provides a tool to ensure that the basic requirements have been addressed and that evidence has been recorded. The most effective audits are those during which auditors simply talk with the auditees to learn everything they can about the process being audited. If auditors work in pairs, the note-taker is responsible for recording the evidence in the appropriate place while the question-asker is learning everything possible about the process. Using this "conversational" style of auditing will make everyone in the process more comfortable and will uncover more breakdowns in the quality management system than simply reading off a checklist.

Although the advantages of the conversational style of auditing are clear, it can also encourage the auditor to pursue issues that far exceed the original scope of the audit. The auditor may start out auditing the purchasing process and end up in Shipping, out of breath, before the day is over. Exceeding the scope of the audit uses up valuable time to pursue issues for which the auditor did not adequately prepare. When the auditor suspects that there may be issues in need of attention beyond the scope of the audit, he or she should pass this information along to the management representative or audit coordinator. An additional audit of the other process may be scheduled, if necessary, to pursue the issue.

Issue an audit report within 24 hours of the audit.

A common problem in an organization's internal audit process is the lack of timely, thorough corrective action. Though the auditor is not responsible for the corrective action, there are four things he or she can do to encourage timely, thorough corrective action. These will be discussed in Chapter 7. One of those items is to issue the report within 24 hours of the audit.

If the report is issued several weeks after an audit, it will typically be filed in the manager's "to be done" pile. The discussion of findings has faded and exactly what the auditor is saying is less clear. Even the most conscientious manager, who intended to call the auditor for further clarification, seldom makes the call. It almost never happens.

The audit report should be issued immediately while discussions are still fresh. Corrective action assignments should be made soon thereafter. The audit reporting process is discussed further in Chapter 7.

Hold a closing meeting to review audit findings.

The audit report should be handed out at the closing meeting. It is this author's experience that not having a closing meeting is equivalent to having no corrective action. The closing meeting is where the manager of the area audited questions each finding for understanding and for validity. The manager should fully understand each finding and why it is a finding by the end of the closing meeting so that he or she can immediately initiate the corrective action.

Now, let's discuss each of the auditor's responsibilities in more detail.

5

Audit Preparation

Preparing for the internal audit is the most critical phase of the audit process. Unless your organization is fortunate enough to have a full-time audit staff, each auditor typically performs only one to three audits a year. To develop the confidence needed to ensure that the process will be thoroughly evaluated, auditors must know in advance what evidence they will be looking for, how many records they will need to review, and what they will be looking for when they review the records. They must also anticipate audit trails that will allow them to evaluate the interactions between processes.

If you carefully instructed me on the process of machining a part, I might be able to machine a part that met specifications. But if you asked me six months later to machine that part, I doubt that I could produce something that resembled your requirements unless you either provided good refresher training or very effective job aides. Yet we often ask internal auditors to perform effective audits months after they have received the training without providing adequate tools to ensure their success. This chapter will focus not only on a step-by-step preparation process, but also on providing internal auditors with the necessary tools and techniques to enable effective audits.

An effective audit preparation process includes seven steps:

Step 1: Define and understand the scope of the audit

Step 2: Review applicable standards

Step 3: Prepare a process models

Step 4: Review applicable documentation

Step 5: Review previous audit results

Step 6: Create an effective checklist

Step 7: Perform a pre-audit meeting

This chapter will discuss each step in the preparation of an internal audit.

STEP 1: DEFINE AND UNDERSTAND THE SCOPE OF THE AUDIT

Defining the scope of the audit was discussed in Chapter 4. The management representative or audit coordinator is typically responsible for defining the scope of each audit and communicating that scope to the auditors. The audit may cover the entire organization; all processes related to a specific area, department, or product; or a specific process within the quality management system. This book will focus primarily on the process-based audit, but the concepts introduced may be applicable to any type of internal audit.

It is the auditors' responsibility to ensure that they understand the scope of the audit before they begin the preparation process. The audit matrix provided in Appendix D is an excellent tool to communicate which process is being audited and which areas of the facility should be included in the audit.

The management representative or audit coordinator can also provide an "audit package" to further clarify what procedures and clauses of ISO 9001:2008 the auditors are responsible for auditing. The audit package may consist of:

- *Copies of procedures or other documentation to be audited.*
  Though these procedures must be the current revision, they should not be the "controlled copies;" the auditors will highlight them and write on them as they prepare for their audit. This documentation can be destroyed after the audit or filed with the audit records.

- *A copy of the backbone checklist(s) for the process to be audited.*
  The auditors will reword this checklist and expand it based on their review of relevant documentation.

- *Results from previous audits.* Auditors must be aware of previous audit findings so that they can verify the effectiveness of the corrective action taken.

Having defined and understood the scope of the audit, the auditor is now ready to review the appropriate clauses of ISO 9001:2008 and any other applicable standards.

STEP 2: REVIEW APPLICABLE STANDARDS

Auditors should perform a careful review of the requirements of each standard against which they will be auditing. Many internal audits are conducted against ISO 9001:2008, but other standards may also apply to an organization. The scope should clearly define the applicable standards as well as the sections of those standards that apply to the audit. (See Appendix E for a description of the new requirements in ISO 9001:2008.)

In studying the standard, the auditor may choose to highlight the word "shall" each time it appears. This will allow the auditor to focus on one requirement at a time to ensure that he or she understands its meaning. It will also make it easier to verify that processes conform to all requirements of the standard.

If requirements are ambiguous or unclear, the auditor should seek clarification before continuing the preparation process. ISO 9000:2005 is an excellent resource for definitions of terms used in ISO 9001:2008. ISO 9004 is a good source of information for the internal auditor. Although the registrar cannot hold an organization accountable to the content of ISO 9004, it will assist in understanding of the requirements of ISO 9001:2008. This document is intended to be a guideline to move the organization beyond the basic requirements of ISO 9001. It is also a useful tool for understanding process methodology. The management representative or audit coordinator is typically another resource for clarifying the requirements of ISO 9001.

STEP 3: PREPARE A PROCESS MODEL

When the auditor understands the requirements of both the standard and the organization's documentation, he or she will prepare a process model. If process models were developed as a part of the organization's documentation, they will be reviewed at this step. If process models were not developed as part of the quality system implementation, the auditor may choose to review documentation (see Step 4) before creating the process models themselves. Understanding the inputs and outputs of a process is fundamental to performing a good process-based audit.

To prepare a process model, first identify the outputs (desired results) of the process. Then identify those inputs that feed into the process being audited. These typically represent interfaces with other processes in the organization. Process models may be depicted in any way that works for an organization. This text will define the inputs in terms of four major categories:

- Given the desired results of the process, what METRICS are maintained to determine the effectiveness of the process?

- WHO participates in the process?

- What INFORMATION is needed to perform the process effectively? (This category will include any procedures, work instructions, and so on that relate to the process as well as any other information that is required for the process to operate effectively.)

- WHAT parts, materials, equipment, tools, hardware and software are required for this process?

To illustrate the process model, consider a manufacturing process. The desired output is typically acceptable product produced on time at a competitive cost (that is, minimal scrap or rework). Records may also be defined as outputs of a process. Records may include completed batch sheets, operator log sheets, and in-process inspection forms or electronic records such as DCS reports, electronic SPC charts, or any other evidence of conformance to specified requirements.

Inputs into a manufacturing process may include:

- METRICS:
  - Scrap rates
  - First-pass rates
  - Rework
  - Delivery performance
  - Productivity rates
- WHO:
  - Competent operators
  - Competent supervisors
  - Competent process engineers
- INFORMATION:
  - User-friendly work instructions
  - Prints/drawings
  - Visual aids
  - Production schedules
  - Batch sheets
  - Product specifications
  - Process specifications
  - Packaging standards
- WHAT parts, materials, tools, equipment, hardware, software:
  - Raw materials or incoming components that arrive on time and meet the organization's specifications
  - Well-maintained process equipment
  - Accurate instrumentation
  - Appropriate tools
  - Process control software

Processes will differ according to the industry and organization. To further illustrate the process methodology, sample process models for the following common processes have been provided in Appendix A of this book:

- Management review
- Training
- Maintenance
- Customer-related processes (definition and review of customer requirements)
- Design and development control
- Purchasing
- Production (or service provision)
- Calibration (control of monitoring and measuring equipment)
- Customer satisfaction
- Internal quality audit
- Monitoring and measurement of product
- Corrective action
- Preventive action

These process models have also been provided on a CD so that they can be easily customized to fit your organization. These models are generic in nature and must be revised as necessary to fit the specific components of an organization's quality management system. Once defined for your organization, they may be used as audit tools for future audit teams.

The effectiveness of the process can then be evaluated using the process model as a starting point.

Is the process effective in providing desired or expected results? (METRICS box)

What metrics are being maintained that would indicate the effectiveness of the process? (These should be recorded in the METRICS box on the process model.) For a manufacturing process, these may include productivity, on-time delivery, first pass rate, scrap rate, rework, and so on. For a purchasing process, they may include on-time arrival of purchased parts and materials, reject rate at receiving, and so on. Examples of potential metrics are provided for each process in Appendix A. These metrics can be evaluated to determine the effectiveness of the process in achieving the desired or expected results. If these metrics have not been developed, the auditor must evaluate how the effectiveness can be determined.

Have required inputs been clearly defined? (WHO, INFORMATION, and WHAT boxes)

A common reason that process inputs are not adequate to ensure the effective implementation of the process is that the input requirements have simply never been clearly defined.

The lack of well-defined input requirements is a common source of findings that can generate return on investment. In one of several examples where I found that Purchasing was not receiving production schedules in time to meet suppliers' lead times (production schedules might be listed in the INFORMATION category), the cause of the problem was found to be the lack of clearly communicated needs and expectations of the buyer. The Production Scheduler had the ability to get an estimated schedule to the buyer several weeks in advance. He simply did not know the buyer needed it then. This finding led to cost savings related to premium freight, lost production time, and unnecessary product changeovers.

An input of the training process is well-defined competence requirements for each position affecting product quality. Training may be lacking in an area because competence requirements have not been defined. New employees are left to learn through their mistakes. Depending upon the position, these mistakes can be quite costly. Poorly defined competence requirements and training needs in Maintenance can lead to excessive downtime and higher costs related to spare parts, scrap, and rework. Poorly defined training needs in Sales can lead to orders being accepted that manufacturing or servicing simply cannot meet, poorly defined customer requirements, and dissatisfied customers. The ultimate results are excessive production costs, more premium freight, and lost business.

Are employees getting the inputs they need to ensure that desired results can be achieved?

Even when input requirements are well defined, the inputs may not be adequate to meet the needs of the auditee.

Examples of process inputs not meeting the needs of the user might include:

- Prints and specifications with tolerances that are illegible or that cannot be met by the current manufacturing process (INFORMATION box)

- Schedules that cannot be met by production (INFORMATION box)

- Training requirements that focus primarily on human resource issues (for example, how to schedule vacation time, how to call in sick, and so on) and omit job-specific training issues (WHO box)

- Equipment with a history of excessive downtime (WHAT box)

- Software programs that are cumbersome, difficult to understand, and inadequate to meet the needs of the user (WHAT box)

- Poorly calibrated instrumentation (WHAT box)

- Inadequately defined customer requirements (INFORMATION box)

- Poorly designed customer satisfaction survey results that do not provide adequate information to initiate corrective or preventive actions (INFORMATION box)

These are all examples of interfaces that have broken down between processes. Where these problems exist, corrective action will typically involve a team of employees representing the applicable processes to resolve the problem. Internal audits can be used as the motivation to address these issues and effectively resolve them.

Are responsibilities and authorities clearly defined and understood? (WHO box)

The lack of clearly defined responsibilities and authorities is at the root of about a fourth to a third of findings in the audits that I perform. As organizations strive to streamline and simplify their documented processes, defined responsibilities and authorities are typically the first detail to be eliminated. When organizations restructure and reorganize, clear responsibilities and authorities may not be adequately defined for the new positions.

The auditor should verify that responsibilities and authorities are clearly spelled out in any available documentation. If they are not defined in documents provided for review, the auditor will need to explore this issue. During the audit, the auditor should verify that responsibilities and authorities are clearly understood and communicated.

Depending on the process being audited, examples of responsibilities and authorities that are often not clearly defined include:

- Who follows up on supplier corrective action when the supplier does not respond?

- Who compares receiving inspection results to established specifications when a shipment arrives?

- Who verifies the effectiveness of corrective actions?

- Who monitors websites for potential inquiries from customers?

- Who receives production/service data and what action is expected based on the data?

- Who tracks action items following a management review?

Has the process been clearly established and documented where necessary? (INFORMATION box)

ISO 9001:2008 takes some emphasis off documentation requirements by specifying only six required procedures:

- Control of documents

- Control of records

- Internal audits

- Control of nonconforming product

- Corrective action

- Preventive action

But requirement 4.2.1.d goes on to say that the organization must have additional documentation as required to control the processes within their quality management system. Where skills can be taught and verified during the training process, documentation on how to perform that skill is rarely needed. Examples may include reading a micrometer, measuring the length of the product using a tape measure, or reading a print.

Where minimum requirements for a position require some basic certification or degree, the skills that should have been mastered during the certification process need not typically be documented. But often documentation is needed to train these employees on the processes and equipment that are specific to your organization. For example:

- A certified welder would probably not need instructions on general welding techniques, but may need instructions on issues that are specific to your products or equipment.

- A registered nurse (RN) may not need a detailed instruction on how to give a shot, but may need a documented instruction on how to operate the autoclave equipment at your facility.

- A professional engineer (PE) would not need documented instructions on basic engineering concepts, but would typically need documentation describing the print control process or the project management requirements at your organization.

In assessing whether or not adequate documentation exists, a new employee can be a valuable resource. The primary customer of documented procedures is the new employee. This person is then in the best position to evaluate the effectiveness of that documentation. The auditor may ask the following questions:

- Were you trained by the procedures/instructions in this department?

- If so, were they helpful to you?

- If not, why not? Were they too long? Too short? Non-existent? Incorrect?

This information is useful in assessing the adequacy of documentation for that process.

Is the process carried out in accordance with the documentation?

This is the compliance auditing with which we are most familiar. As the auditor reviews available documentation, he or she should highlight those items that warrant verification during the audit (see Step 4). As such, the audit will verify conformance to the documented quality management system as well as to the standard itself. In preparing for the audit, auditors should identify what records they will need to review to verify conformance to the documentation, how many they will want to pull, and what they will be looking for when they pull the records. Process-specific checklists are provided in Appendix B to help auditors ensure that both ISO 9001 requirements and the requirements of the documentation are met.

Do employees operating in this process have appropriate parts, materials, tools, equipment, hardware, and software? (WHAT box)

This category of inputs will consider whether or not employees have the appropriate resources and materials to achieve the desired outputs. Are there repetitive problems relating to incoming parts and materials? Are there any repetitive problems related to equipment and tools? Is any software user-friendly and suitable? Does the organization have the appropriate hardware to run the required software?

Understanding the process model for the process being audited is critical in evaluating the effectiveness of that process. Once thorough process models have been developed, future auditors can use them in their audit preparation. "Prepare a process model" then becomes "review the process model," saving a significant amount of time in the preparation process.

STEP 4: REVIEW APPLICABLE DOCUMENTATION

The auditor must also have a good understanding of the organization's documentation that relates to the process being audited. Though not required by ISO 9001:2008, many organizations develop a quality management system that includes three tiers or layers of documentation:

- *The quality manual.* The quality manual serves as a roadmap to the rest of the system. ISO 9001:2008 requires that the quality manual include:
  - The scope of the quality management system, including any exclusions to ISO 9001:2008 and their justification;

– The supporting procedures, or a reference to those procedures;

– A description of the interaction of the processes in the quality management system.

The manual also typically includes the quality policy and an organization chart or brief description of the organization's structure. It may also include a process map that can be used to understand how the process being audited interacts with other processes in the system.

- *Procedures.* Procedures provide additional information, where required, on the processes in the quality management system. Procedures typically address who will do what and when or how often. Six documented procedures are required by ISO 9001:2008:

  – Control of documents

  – Control of records

  – Internal audit

  – Control of nonconforming product

  – Corrective action

  – Preventive action

  Beyond these six required procedures, however, ISO 9001:2008 requires "documents needed by the organization to ensure the effective planning, operation, and control of its processes" (reference 4.2.1.d).

- *Work instructions.* Work instructions provide more information, where needed, on how specific activities in each process are performed. Work instructions may be in the form of operator instructions, batch sheets, control plans, test methods, calibration instructions, training checklists, audit checklists, raw material specifications, product specifications, drawings, blank forms, and so on.

Those documents related to the process being audited should be defined in the INFORMATION box on the process model.

Some organizations will have a fourth tier of documents that includes the records (reference 4.2.1.e). Records are controlled in an entirely different manner than other documents. Documents in the first three tiers must be readily available and properly approved. They must be the latest issue and there must be some way to indicate that (reference 4.2.3). Records, on the other hand, must simply be filed in a disciplined manner (reference 4.2.4).

The auditor should start the document review with a review of the quality manual. The quality manual will describe the processes at your organization and the interaction of those processes. It should also provide some insight into how the standard has been implemented.

The next step in the document review process is to read, study, and understand any second-tier procedures that may be available for the process being audited. In reading these documents, the auditor may choose to highlight those items that will help create an effective checklist:

- *Flags.* These are requirements in the procedure that make you say, "When donkeys fly." In a new quality management system, flags are created when authors of the procedures start with what they think the process should look like some day versus what it looks like today. In a mature system, flags are created when processes are changed, but documentation has not been updated to reflect that change. Though not always, flags typically indicate that the procedure should be updated to reflect actual practice.

  From the author's perspective, common flags include:
  - "All corrective actions will be closed out in 30 days."
  - "All supplier corrective actions are due back in the Purchasing office within three business days."
  - "The following seventeen signatures are required on each quality procedure."
  - "All eight of the following managers are required to attend each monthly management review meeting."

- *Points to verify.* These are not flags, but requirements the auditor would like to see verified during the audit. Examples include:
  - "The management representative issues an annual internal audit schedule. The schedule ensures that each process in the quality management system and each area in the company are audited every year."
  - "Internal auditors must receive training on the requirements of ISO 9001:2008 and audit techniques. They must then complete two audits with a qualified auditor before being qualified themselves."
  - "The QA Technician samples the product every four hours and performs the following inspections..."
  - "The Quality Manager conducts customer focus groups monthly and forwards results to the Management Representative. The Management Representative analyzes the results and initiates corrective or preventive actions as necessary."

- *Responsibilities and authorities.* From a technical standpoint, the auditor should make note of responsibilities and authorities to ensure that they have been defined as required in section 5.5.1 of ISO 9001:2008. Of course, ISO 9001 does not dictate that these be documented in procedures, but they most often are. If the auditor reads the procedure and does not know who is responsible for performing each activity, this may raise a flag. The auditor should verify during the audit that responsibilities and authorities have indeed been well defined and communicated.

From a practical standpoint, the auditor should highlight responsibilities and authorities so that he or she will know with whom to talk during the audit. If the appropriate person is noted beside each section of questions on the audit checklist, time is saved during the audit that would otherwise be spent locating the right people.

- *Records.* Finally, the auditor should highlight the names of records in order to begin learning the language of the auditee. Asking operators where they record their "quality critical process parameters" is not speaking the correct language. After a good document review, the auditor will know to ask for the "daily log sheet," "DCS parameters," "operator's log sheet," or other documents using terminology the auditee uses. The audit progresses more smoothly for everyone when the auditor knows the language of the auditee.

Depending on the process being audited, the auditor may review some of the third-tier work instructions or blank forms to understand the process and the type of documentation that will be reviewed during the audit. The majority of audit preparation, however, is typically spent studying any available second-tier procedures.

If the process being audited is new to the auditor, the internal auditor may request a pre-audit tour of the area. Other trained auditors who work in that area typically are willing to show the auditor around and briefly explain the process. A pre-audit tour may be quite helpful in understanding the procedures and the process.

STEP 5: REVIEW PREVIOUS AUDIT RESULTS

The auditor should complete the document review process by reviewing the results of previous internal and external audits. The effectiveness of action taken for previous findings can then be evaluated. Repetitive audit findings in a given area may be an indicator that the auditor should focus on that area until the issues have been fully resolved.

STEP 6: CREATE AN EFFECTIVE CHECKLIST

Perhaps the hottest debate in conducting effective internal audits is whether or not the auditor should be given a previously developed checklist of basic questions to use as a guide in the audit process. I believe that we should provide the tools that are necessary for successful audits and that an effective checklist is one of those tools.

As I mentioned earlier in the book, if you thoroughly trained me on how to perform a specific task, I could probably meet your requirements that day. But if you ask me to perform that task for the first time six months later, I seriously doubt that I would be capable of doing an adequate job. Yet we often put our internal auditors in this position.

Unless your organization is fortunate enough to have full-time auditors, your internal auditors may conduct as many as two to four audits a year. These auditors are often asked to squeeze effective auditing into their already loaded list of responsibilities and to perform these audits as long as three to six months after the training was provided. In doing so, we set up our auditors to fail in their attempt to perform thorough audits that reveal specific opportunities to improve the business and result in tangible returns to the bottom line.

Rather than withholding the tools that auditors need to be successful, I believe we must provide those tools and find ways to make them useful in achieving the desired results. Checklists can be designed to fully evaluate conformance to specified standards and documentation and also evaluate the effectiveness of audited processes. But regardless of the checklist design, auditors must remember that checklists are intended to serve as guidelines for the audit and not scripts. The effective use of a checklist is further discussed in Chapter 6.

A "backbone" checklist is a list of questions or evidence that should be included in the audit to verify the effectiveness of a process, conformance to ISO 9001:2008, and conformance to the basic requirements of the organization's documented quality management system. Templates for such checklists are provided in Appendix B of this book and also provided on a CD to facilitate its customization. This checklist is not intended to be used as it is written. It must be customized to include your organization's terminology and requirements. It simply provides a solid basis on which to build.

The first checklist in Appendix B is a list of questions that may be asked when verifying any process. The auditor should review these questions prior to each audit and evaluate which of them would be appropriate to determine the effectiveness of the process. Process-specific checklists are provided for common processes that may be used as a basis for the "conformance" piece of the audit.

There are several advantages to using a well-designed "backbone" checklist during the internal audit. Those advantages are discussed below.

Previously designed "backbone" checklists improve consistency among the auditors. A common complaint of any type of audit is that the results depend more on who the auditor was than on the health of the process. If all auditors are using the same "backbone" checklist, the results will more accurately reflect the effectiveness of the process being audited. Consider, for example, the following question on a checklist.

Pull 10 Corrective Action Requests (CARs) at random and verify the following:

- Was the cause of the problem identified and recorded on the CAR?

- Was action taken that should have eliminated the cause?

- Is there evidence that the action taken was effective?

- Were any associated documents updated as a result of the action taken? (Pull any documents that should have been updated and verify that they have indeed been issued and that affected employees are aware of the change.)

If every auditor used this question as a starting point to verify conformance to the standard and to the organization's own documented procedure, the results of an audit of corrective action would be somewhat consistent. Of course further questions would be necessary to fully verify conformance to ISO 9001:2008 and to verify the effectiveness of the process. See Appendix B for additional sample questions for corrective action.

A well-designed "backbone" checklist ensures thorough coverage of the quality management system. As I audit quality management systems, a common problem I see is that audits do not thoroughly cover the requirements of ISO 9001:2008. If internal auditors are left on their own to create an audit plan from scratch before each audit, the audits become more and more shallow as time constraints become tighter and tighter. The end result is often two or three questions that address a given process. A ten-minute audit of any process typically is not sufficient to fully verify conformance and effectiveness.

Using a good "backbone" checklist, however, enables the auditors to ensure that the process effectively meets the basic requirements of ISO 9001:2008 and the organization's documented quality management system.

A well-designed "backbone" checklist also provides ample space for recording facts and data observed during the audit. A common finding in registration audits is that there is plenty of evidence to support the negative issues found during an audit, but little evidence of processes that were found to be effectively implemented. A well-designed "backbone" checklist provides space to record evidence of the good as well as evidence of the bad. The auditor has not completed the audit until there is evidence recorded for each applicable question.

The biggest benefit of a "backbone" checklist is that it saves significant time in preparing for the audit. Internal auditors often have difficulty finding time to adequately prepare for the audit. As we have discussed, internal auditors are required to read and study the applicable sections of ISO 9001:2008; to review or develop a process model; to read and study applicable procedures or other documentation; to review past internal audit findings; and to create an effective audit plan. It's often difficult to fit these tasks into an already overloaded schedule. Anything we can do to make the internal auditor's job easier and more effective is appreciated by everyone.

I certainly acknowledge the concerns of many that audit checklists are detrimental to the audit process. Let's take a look at some of those concerns.

"Backbone" checklists may cause audits to become stale. The most common reason that I hear for not providing "backbone" checklists is that they cause audits to become stale and discourage adequate preparation. This is a common complaint when the checklist is based on "yes/no" questions or questions that do not require the review of specific records. Most checklists available for purchase can be thoroughly completed without pulling a single record. The really poor checklists are based on "yes/no" questions and ask the auditor only to check "complies" or "does not comply." They don't include space to record specific evidence that was observed during the audit. Examples of such questions include:

- Do you have a corrective action procedure?

- Does it address the identification of the cause of the problem?

- Does it address removing the cause of the problem?

- Does it require that actions taken must be evaluated for effectiveness before they are closed out?

These questions are acceptable for a system audit to verify conformance of the procedures to ISO 9001:2008, but they are inadequate to determine whether or not activities actually conform to the requirements.

Better checklists have questions such as:

- What processes are used to determine the causes of problems?

- Who is responsible for ensuring that actions are taken to eliminate the causes?

- How do you determine whether or not actions taken have been effective?

- What process do you have in place to ensure that any associated documentation is updated based on the actions taken?

These are good questions to verify that processes are in place, but they do not verify that processes conform to ISO 9001:2008 nor do they verify that processes are effective. Both of these checklists will lead to stale audits over the years if the auditors simply read off the checklists.

To overcome the stale audit, we must prepare checklists that are based on process models as well as on facts and data. Good conformance checklists will identify what evidence is to be reviewed, how many samples should be pulled, and what the auditor should look for on the pulled records. Asking these four questions can be effective as long as they are followed with:

"Review 10 CARs at random and verify the following:

- Was the cause of the problem identified and recorded on the CAR?

- Was action taken that should have eliminated the cause?

- Is there evidence that the action taken was effective?

- Were any associated documents updated as a result of the action taken? (Review any documents that should have been updated and verify that they have indeed been issued and that affected employees are aware of the change.)"

These questions will prevent the audit process from becoming stale because different records will be pulled each year to verify that the corrective action process is in conformance with specified requirements. Then the auditor will use the process model to formulate questions to verify the effectiveness of the process. The full process for developing effective checklists is described later in this chapter.

Using a "backbone" checklist discourages adequate preparation. I agree with this argument. At some point during the life of the audit process, the "backbone" checklist will become very thorough. It will be tempting for the auditor to simply read from this checklist to do the audit. And, indeed, they will do a decent audit. But to completely verify the effectiveness of the process being audited, the auditor should follow each of the preparation steps outlined above. When the "backbone" checklist has evolved into a highly effective internal audit tool, the management representative or audit coordinator should follow up with each auditor before the audit to see what types of things they highlighted during their document review and what questions they added to their "backbone" checklist. Doing so will ensure that the auditors have adequately prepared for their audit.

Using a "backbone" checklist encourages auditors to read a list of questions rather than explore audit trails that may come up in an audit. This is probably the strongest argument against audit checklists. Auditors must not use the checklist as a script. The checklist is intended to be a guide for the audit, to help auditors prepare for appropriate trails, and to allow for the recording of observations noted. Auditors must be appropriately trained to go beyond the checklist to explore potential issues; they must not limit themselves to those questions provided. I acknowledge that the danger exists of depending too much on the checklist. But I have found that the alternative, of not providing this guide, is more detrimental for the internal audit process.

So what is the ultimate resolution? Again, I recommend that a "backbone" checklist be provided to the internal auditor, and that the following rules be used with it:

- Checklists must be based on the process methodology—verifying the adequacy of inputs into a process and the effectiveness of the outputs. It must not be a simple list of "shalls" from the standard that have been reworded into questions.

- Checklists should include those interfaces with other processes that may lead an auditor to explore audit trails.

- Checklists should be based on facts and data and not on "yes/no" questions or open-ended questions only.

- Checklists should be used by the auditor as a guideline to the audit and not as a script. The checklist should not be read to the auditee. See Chapter 6 for a further discussion on the effective use of a checklist during the actual audit.

How do you develop an effective "backbone" checklist?

A good audit checklist is the most valuable tool your organization can develop to encourage successful internal audits.

There are some questions that should be asked in most, if not all, process-based audits. These are more specifically defined in the "All Processes" checklist found at the beginning of Appendix B. Questions for each category of inputs include:

- METRICS:
  - What metrics are maintained to determine whether or not this process is effective?
  - Who looks at these metrics?
  - How are metrics evaluated? Do you have defined goals or objectives?
  - Are you meeting your goals? If not, may I see the action plans you are using to achieve them?

- WHO:
  - Who participates in this process?
  - Have responsibilities and authorities been clearly defined for these personnel?
  - Have competence requirements been defined for each of these positions?
  - Is training provided to ensure that competence requirements are met?
  - May I see the training records for each of the following new employees in this process? (Verify that training met the competence requirements and that records of training are complete.)

- How do you evaluate the effectiveness of training? (Follow the trail to verify that training for new employees in a position was effective. Interview new employees to evaluate their perception of the effectiveness of the training process.)

- INFORMATION:
  - What procedures or instructions are used in this process? (These may include procedures, operator work instructions, test methods, calibration methods, prints, drawings, product specifications, raw material specifications, batch sheets, and so on.)
  - May I see them please? (Verify that documentation is readily available, properly approved, and current. The auditor may use the "Document Control Audit Matrix" in Appendix B to record results.)
  - Is this documentation suitable to meet the needs of the user? Is it useful? If not, why not? Is it too long? Too short? Dead wrong? Obsolete?
  - What other information is needed for this process? (Depending on the process being audited, this may include production schedules, inventory levels, purchase requisitions, work orders, test requirements, pick lists, shipping schedules, and so on.)
  - Do you receive this information in a timely manner? Is it accurate? Is it complete?

- PARTS, MATERIALS, EQUIPMENT, TOOLS, HARDWARE, SOFTWARE:
  - What parts, materials, equipment, tools, hardware, or software are required for this process?
  - Are there any repetitive problems associated with these?
  - Are they available when you need them?

Most of these questions would be applicable for any process. The auditor would then add questions that are more specific to the process being audited. Again, a series of these more process-specific checklists is provided in Appendix B of this book as well as on the enclosed CD.

The first audit team for each process can help develop the first round of "backbone" checklists. The checklists will then be refined with each subsequent audit. After three or four rounds of audits, the "backbone" checklist becomes a powerful tool for verifying conformance of the process to specified requirements and the effectiveness of the process in achieving the desired results.

After completing a thorough document review, the first step in developing a good "backbone" checklist is to eliminate those questions that do not apply to the process being audited or to the organization's QMS. For example, in the "All Processes" checklist many of the questions related to the "PARTS, MATERIALS, EQUIPMENT, TOOLS, HARDWARE, SOFTWARE" box do not relate to management system processes—that is, to management review, corrective action, and so on. Those questions would be deleted for those audits. The auditor should then reword remaining questions to incorporate your organization's specific terminology.

The checklist provided in Appendix B uses a combination of questions to define the requirements to be reviewed in the audit. Audit matrices within the checklists may be used to collect and record data for specific records that are pulled. Each process begins with a broad, open question to get the auditee talking to the auditor. Audit matrices may be used to provide the auditor an opportunity to easily record the evidence that was observed. The matrix provides instruction regarding which record to pull and what to look for when the record is pulled.

Using matrices to record audit results saves significant time in the audit process and ensures that adequate records of audit activities are maintained. Some cells in the audit matrix are split. (Reference the "Document Control" matrix at the end of the "All Processes" checklist.) The top half of the split cells may be completed during the preparation process to indicate what the procedure requires for that item. In the document control matrix, for example, the approval column contains split cells. The auditors can record in the top half who has the authority to approve each document. In doing so, the auditor has all the information he or she needs without having to fumble through procedures during the audit. The results of the audit can then be recorded in the bottom half of the cell (that is, how many of the documents observed during the audit were approved by the correct person).

When starting with any generic audit checklist, an auditor should follow the steps below to ensure that the checklist adequately represents your specific organization and its quality management system.

Reword each question on the checklist to incorporate your organization's specific terminology.

Using a generic checklist without customizing it to reflect the terminology and practices of a specific organization is a mistake that will inevitably lead to unsuccessful audits. The auditees—and even the auditors—often do not understand the questions in the checklist or the types of records that should be evaluated.

The number of records to be pulled must be customized to meet the needs of the organization. There is no minimum sample size requirement, but the general rule of thumb for management system audits is a sample size of three to ten combined with a lot of common sense. Common sense should consider:

- How many samples there are to choose from
- How long it will take to audit a single sample

If your organization performs annual management reviews, for example, auditing meeting minutes for three management reviews would be a bit excessive. The appropriate sample size in this situation would be one. If you were auditing the complete traceability of an airplane wing, three would again be a bit excessive considering the time it would take to complete a thorough audit of one sample.

If the record being pulled is the primary record for the entire audit, the auditor will probably want to pull ten samples. For example, in an audit of the corrective action process, CARs will be the primary record to be evaluated. Auditing ten CARs would not be unreasonable.

Minimal sample sizes should be determined during the checklist development phase. As the audit is conducted, the auditor may decide to increase the sample size if necessary to determine the extent of a finding.

In order to practice rewording a generic checklist to fit the unique terminology of an organization, please review the maintenance procedure that has been provided in Appendix C of this book. You may choose to print these documents from the enclosed CD in order to have them in front of you as we customize the "Maintenance" checklist for the specific maintenance process at Acme.

The "All Processes" checklist would be slightly refined for the maintenance process at Acme. See Appendix C of this book for an example of how the "All Processes" checklist might be revised for the Maintenance process at Acme. See Appendix C for an example of how the "All Processes" and "Maintenance-specific" checklists might be reworded for Acme.

Add questions to the checklist from the document review.

Having highlighted those requirements in the procedures that you thought warranted verification will facilitate this process. If the checklist does not already incorporate the highlighted items, add questions in the appropriate places to address those issues.

There may be a number of issues that auditors would like to verify during the audit. These questions should be added to the customized "backbone" checklist before each audit. These additional questions, which do not appear on the standard checklist, will help keep the audit process fresh over the years.

Review the process model and ensure that the checklist adequately addresses whether or not inputs are adequate to achieve desired results.

An example of a model for a maintenance process is provided in Appendix A of this book. Some questions that might be added to that process model include:

- Do work orders include the information you need to effectively and efficiently resolve the problem? (INFORMATION box)

- How often do you go to the stock room to get equipment parts and find that those parts are not available? How often must you keep production equipment down until those parts can be obtained? (WHAT box)

Based on these steps, the new "backbone" checklist for Acme's maintenance process is included at the end of Appendix C.

Extensive customization was required to make this maintenance checklist fit the terminology and requirements of Acme manufacturing. You will find that more customization is needed in some sections than in others. Management review, design and development control, internal audits, and corrective action, for example, will typically need minimal alteration. Defining and reviewing customer requirements, purchasing, and process control typically will need more extensive customization. It is critical that the "backbone" checklist you develop include the specific terminology and requirements of your organization if your internal audits are to be effective.

The preceding discussion on creating an effective internal audit checklist primarily focused on the first round of internal audits. Once an effective "backbone" checklist has been established, this step becomes, "Review the 'backbone' checklist for understanding. Reword any questions that need clarification. Add questions to the checklist from your highlighted procedures." This will save significant time in audit preparation.

STEP 7: CONDUCT A PRE-AUDIT MEETING

Just prior to the audit, the supervisor or manager of the primary area being audited should review with employees information that is critical to the audit. Employees need to know:

- What is ISO 9001:2008 and why is it important to our organization? Be specific. Do customers require registration for future business? Does the organization see the quality management system as a means to improve the business? If so, what successes have already been experienced? If return on investment has been calculated for previous audit results, this should be shared with the employees.

- When will the audit take place? What will be the audit agenda?

- What will employees be expected to know? Employees should know that they will be expected to understand the quality policy and objectives and how their activities affect the organization's ability to meet those objectives. This is a good opportunity to review what those objectives are and to provide employees a review of the organization's progress toward meeting those objectives. Employees will also need to know where their documentation is located and how to use that documentation. Finally, employees need to know their jobs. They must understand that "I do not know" is an acceptable response in an audit. It may be that the auditor is simply asking the wrong person.

- How open should employees be during the audit? For internal audits, remind employees that they are the customers of the audit process. If processes are not working correctly in the area, recording them in the audit report may be the incentive that brings appropriate attention to the problem. Of course, if this briefing is provided prior to an external audit, employees should be advised to "answer the question honestly and thoroughly, then wait for the next question."

This information can be reviewed in departmental meetings, department announcements, via e-mail, or even on a communication board. To encourage the supervisor or manager to discuss this information with employees, the management representative or audit coordinator may provide a talk sheet with preprinted questions and answers.

SUMMARY OF AUDIT PREPARATION

To summarize the audit preparation phase, let's review the specific steps to be followed in preparing for the *first* audit of a specific process.

Step 1: Define and understand the scope of the audit.

- What process(es) will be covered in this audit? What sections of ISO 9001:2008 relate to these processes?

- What procedures or other documentation are applicable to this process?

- What areas of the organization will the auditor visit in order to ensure that the audit scope is thoroughly covered?

Step 2: Read, study, and understand the applicable sections of ISO 9001:2008.

Step 3: Develop and review a process model.

- Identify the desired process results or outputs.
- Identify the inputs into the process.

Step 4: Read, study, and understand applicable documentation.

- Compare to the standard for conformance.
- Highlight those items that you would like to verify during the audit. These may include flags, points to verify, responsibilities, and the names of records.

Step 5: Review previous audit results.

Step 6: Create an effective "backbone" checklist.

- Start with the checklist provided in Appendix B.
- Eliminate those questions that do not apply to your audit.
- Reword each remaining question to incorporate your organization's specific terminology.
- Add questions to the checklist from the document review and review of previous audits.
- Review the process model and ensure that the checklist adequately addresses whether or not inputs are adequate to achieve desired results.

Step 7: Conduct a pre-audit meeting.

The preparation phase in subsequent audits of each process will be similar but much less time consuming.

Step 1: Define and understand the scope of the audit.

- What sections of ISO 9001:2008 should be covered in the audit?
- What procedures or other documentation are applicable to this process?
- What areas of the organization will the auditor visit in order to ensure that the audit scope is thoroughly covered?

Step 2: Read, study, and understand the applicable sections of ISO 9001:2008.

Step 3: Review the applicable process model for understanding.

Step 4: Read, study, and understand applicable documentation.

- Compare to the standard for conformance.

- Highlight those items that you would like to verify during the audit. These may include flags, points to verify, responsibilities, and the names of records.

Step 5: Review previous audit results.

Step 6: Review the "backbone" checklist for understanding.

- Reword any questions that need clarification.

- Add questions to the checklist from your highlighted procedures.

Step 7: Conduct a pre-audit meeting.

Using this disciplined approach to audit preparation will increase the confidence level of the internal auditor and all but ensure the success of the audit.

6

Performing the Audit

The critical stage of an effective internal audit has already been completed. If the auditors have thoroughly prepared for the audit, they should know what records will be reviewed, how many will be reviewed, and what will be evaluated on those records. In addition, the auditor should have developed a strategy to evaluate the effectiveness of the process being audited. Conducting the audit then becomes an exercise of completing the audit plan while treating the auditees with dignity and respect.

THE "GROUP" OPENING MEETING

Each audit should begin with a brief opening meeting with as many of the auditees present as possible. The purpose of the opening meeting is to establish the environment of the audit. The lead auditor should chair the opening meeting, which typically includes the following agenda:

- The purpose of the audit

- The audit plan

- The time and location of the closing meeting

- Questions from the auditees

For an internal audit, the "group" opening meeting can be as formal or as informal as is appropriate for the size and culture of the organization. For small organizations where employees know each other well, the opening meeting may be simply a five-minute gathering in the department to assure that everyone is aware of the audit, of its purpose and its agenda. In a large organization or in organizations where internal auditors are used from other site locations, the opening meeting should be a more formal event—typically conducted in a conference room or meeting area. Regardless of the formality, the opening meeting should not take more than 10 to 15 minutes.

THE "INDIVIDUAL" OPENING MEETING

In the internal audit, the "individual" opening meeting is the more critical of the two. If the auditor approaches an auditee and immediately begins asking questions related to the audit, the auditee typically will not know the answer to the first several questions. His or her mind probably was on something else entirely when the auditor approached. Auditees may need just a moment to transition to the audit. This is an excellent time to ensure one-on-one that the auditee is comfortable with the purpose of the audit.

Clearly restate the purpose of the audit and invite questions from the auditee.

If the auditee feels that ISO 9001 is just a collection of useless paperwork, provide an opportunity to express that feeling. From a personal standpoint, my heart leaps out of my chest when an angry auditee expresses that emotion. I know that I am about to pull the individual onto the audit team. And that is my goal. I cannot complete an effective audit without his or her expertise on the process.

In helping a client with a recent internal audit, I introduced myself to the auditee, explained the purpose of the audit, and asked if he had any questions about ISO 9001 or the audit process. He angrily replied that ISO 9001 was the most useless pile of junk he had ever experienced on the job. (This is the printable translation of his comments.) Furthermore, he said it was actually costing him money out of his own wallet!

Here's why: Operations personnel are paid at this facility based on quotas. If an employee exceeds the quota for his position, he earns bonus pay. Before the implementation of the ISO 9001 requirements, this operator had made a significant bonus in each paycheck. But since the requirements had been fully implemented, he often failed even to meet his quota.

Having helped companies implement the requirements of ISO 9001 for more than fifteen years, I am fully aware of an organization's tendency to over-document their system. This situation is only one of the detrimental effects of an over-documented process. When I hear such an emotional response to ISO 9001, I know that there is an opportunity to use this audit to simplify the process being audited, create a believer in the internal audit process, and increase the profitability of the organization.

After explaining that it was never the intent of ISO 9001 to decrease productivity and to frustrate the workforce with worthless paperwork, I asked the auditee for his help in explaining where the organization might have become "overly enthusiastic" in implementing the requirements of ISO 9001. Suddenly I had seventeen assistant auditors. Each operator joined the audit process, bringing to me the forms they had to complete on a daily basis and showing me numerous examples of where the same information was being recorded in two or three places or more. As a result of the audit, we were able to take the 27 forms required in this simple manufacturing process and turn them into two forms—one on the front end of the line and one on the back end.

The bottom line in this organization is that process and quality engineers still receive the information they need to reduce quality failures and to increase productivity, but the method was optimized so that operations personnel could see the value and participate in the improvement process. Everyone came out of the audit a winner. Though this organization does not calculate return on investment for their audit findings, I would estimate that the increased productivity as a result of this audit generated at least six figures on the bottom line.

Though the quantity of paperwork in this example was a bit unusual, having the auditee express frustration with the process and using the audit to deal with those frustrations, if possible, is not unusual at all. If the auditee is given an opportunity at the beginning of the audit to ask questions about the management system and the audit process, the auditor may learn critical information about how that audit can be used to improve the business. Again, the auditee is the expert on the process and typically knows where the opportunities for improvement lie. Give him or her a chance to tell you.

Invite the auditee to read the notes taken during the audit and correct any errors.

When I write the word "audit" on a flipchart pad at the beginning of my internal audit classes and ask participants to yell out their first thoughts, as stated earlier I often hear comments such as: "IRS!" "Pink slip!" "Vacation day!" "Fear!" and "Somebody else coming out here telling me how to do my job!" Several years ago, one gentleman yelled out "Clipboard!" That insight spoke volumes to me. Staring at the backside of a clipboard as an auditor takes copious notes is probably the most intimidating, disrespectful aspect of most audits.

If two auditors are used, the note-taker should sit or stand in such a way that the auditee can easily read the notes as they are taken. The auditors should then explain that these notes belong to the entire audit team—including the auditee. The auditee should be invited to read the notes and bring to the attention of the auditors anything that is incorrect or misunderstood.

I learned this lesson early in my audit career. During my very first QMS audit as a Supplier Engineer, I asked a lab technician at a supplier's facility, "Do you calibrate your instruments?" He responded, "No." I had uncovered my first major finding! I dutifully recorded on the checklist clutched to my chest that the organization had no calibration process.

There are a number of things wrong with this picture. This was not one of my more effective opening questions. I had intended to ask whether or not the organization had a calibration process. But because I did not word the question correctly, the technician assumed I was asking if he calibrated the instruments. The first question or statement should be broad and open ended, designed to inspire the auditee to talk to you. I should have said, "Please explain the calibration process here at XYZ Company." I would have learned a lot more about the process.

Had I allowed the auditee to read my notes—and even invited him to do so—I would have avoided that embarrassing moment at the closing meeting when I announced to management that the organization had no calibration process. The managers looked at each other with confused expressions and replied, "We have a reputable company down the street calibrate our instruments once a month. Is that not acceptable to you?"

Inviting the auditee to read the audit notes shows respect for his or her expertise; it will also prevent incorrect audit findings.

Describe the auditee as the customer of the audit process; during the audit, invite him or her to raise any issues that may need attention.

Even after conducting employee awareness training, the pre-audit meeting, and the opening meeting of the audit itself, I often hear auditees tell me that the purpose of an internal audit is to catch them doing something wrong. Take one more opportunity to express to the auditees that they are the customers of the audit and that it may be to their advantage to report process breakdowns so that they can be addressed.

Depending on the concerns of the auditee, the "individual" opening meeting typically takes about five minutes or less. It is time well spent to ensure the success of the audit.

INTERVIEW TECHNIQUES

After the environment of the audit has been well established, the interview can begin. If an auditee is visibly nervous about the process even after the "individual" opening meeting, take a few additional moments to put him or her at ease.

If the auditees appear nervous, consider that they may be reflecting what they see in the auditor. What is your posture? Are you on the edge of your seat and invading someone's personal space? Are you standing with an aggressive posture? Take just a moment to evaluate whether or not you may be inadvertently causing the tension.

Spend a moment talking about something that the auditee finds interesting. In an internal audit, for example, you may know the auditee's hobbies and interests. Take a moment to talk about them.

As a last resort, ask the auditee if he or she has already had a break. Go to a cafeteria, a break room, or some other non-threatening location for a cup of coffee. During the "break," talk about the types of things you will be looking for during the audit. In doing so, you will prepare the auditee and make him or her feel more confident about the ability to contribute to its success. Time is often your greatest enemy in an audit, but spending a few moments putting the auditee at ease is time well spent.

Then just learn everything you can about the process being audited. Start with a broad, open question or statement to get the auditee talking to you:

- "Can you walk me through this process?"

- "Please explain to me how this works."

- "Help me understand the concerns you have about this process (if concerns were raised during the opening meeting)."

Throughout the interview, follow up with records and other documentation to verify conformance to ISO 9001:2008 and conformance to the organization's documented system. Use the audit checklist to record the results of the audit.

If a nonconformance is discovered during the interview, immediately bring it to the auditee's attention as tactfully as possible:

- "I am looking for the design review minutes, but I can't find them. Am I missing something, or were the minutes not maintained?"

- "It looks as though this Purchase Order was issued to a supplier that has not yet been approved."

- "Let's get that down so we can address it one way or the other."

Try to avoid emotional words such as *discrepancy, failure,* or *nonconformance*. Keep the environment positive—focused on the corrective action, not the finding.

At the end of the interview, summarize with the auditee the good findings as well as those that require corrective action. The auditee should not be caught off guard at the closing meeting. Be sure that any finding or concern has been discussed prior to that time.

BASIC COMMUNICATION SKILLS

Basic communication skills are essential to good internal auditing. But good communication skills are difficult to cultivate. It has been said that only 10 percent of communication is completed using words. Other components of communication, and how they affect the internal audit, are discussed below.

Tone of voice.

Tone of voice communicates a lot, whether or not we intend that message to be conveyed. Consider the expression, "You are kidding." Without hearing the speaker's tone of voice, the listener cannot know if this is an expression of total disbelief, great excitement, or something in between.

In an audit situation, the auditee may hear something in the auditor's tone of voice that was not intended. Communication is not complete until you repeat in your own words what you think someone said and the speaker agrees with you. While trying to understand what the auditee was explaining, I used to say, "So you are telling me that you..." I could not understand why auditees were offended by that response until someone asked why I would question his integrity. Apparently the tone in my voice conveyed something other than what I had intended.

If an auditee becomes defensive or aggressive during the audit, the auditor should be aware that he or she might have said something that was simply misunderstood. Think back over the conversation and try to resolve the issue.

Facial expressions.

Facial expressions can communicate thoughts during an audit that the auditor would not necessarily want communicated. Having worked with a number of youth groups through the years, my husband and I have learned to teach new adult advisors to look in the mirror every morning and practice that empathetic "I hear you" expression. If you have not yet mastered that one, the utterly shocked "Have you lost your mind?" expression comes out before you know it and you lose the confidence of the teen.

The same concept applies in auditing. In helping a client in the automotive industry with internal auditing, I approached several welders. The part they were working on was a safety-critical part that could greatly affect an individual's health in specific situations. It appeared to me that they had no process parameters available to monitor during the welding process, so I was curious how they verified the adequacy of the weld. When I asked, they carefully explained to me that they would try to physically pull the pieces apart. If they could pull it apart, it went into the rework bin. If they could not pull it apart, the part passed. It took years of audit experience to squash my "Have you lost your mind?" look.

The organization had never communicated to the welders the importance of that weld. If I had allowed my emotion to show in my expression, it probably would have inadvertently communicated that I thought the welders themselves were to blame for not understanding the critical nature of their work. But lack of adequate communication and training and the lack of adequate process controls were the causes of the problem, certainly not the intelligence level of the workforce.

The auditor should be careful that his or her expression does not shut down the auditee.

Body language, gestures, and posture.

Body language, gestures, and posture can also communicate unintended messages during an audit. I have learned much through the years by asking my clients to critique my audit style after an audit. I have learned, for example, that I tend to sit on the edge of my chair. In most situations, this posture is not a problem. But when I am auditing, it tends to make the auditee feel that I am being overly aggressive. I have learned to put the small of my back in the back of the chair when I sit down during the audit. It creates a more relaxed environment for everyone.

Auditors may also communicate an aggressive position through body language. Standing with one leg cocked out and the clipboard propped on the other hip can create an intimidating environment.

Ignoring the auditee.

It is easy during an audit to think about so many things at one time that you miss what the auditee is saying. Our brains are wired in such a way that when we think back about something we recently learned, our eyes tend to move up and away. It can be irritating to auditees when the auditor does not pay attention to what they are saying. Be aware that when you think back, you may lose eye contact with the auditee. If you are aware of that tendency, it will help you prevent losing track of the conversation.

In an audit where the tension levels may be high, the auditor should be aware of how his or her communication style may be interpreted.

KEYS TO LISTENING

Careful listening is a critical skill that an auditor must develop. Obstacles must be overcome in order to truly hear what the auditee is trying to say.

Failure to separate the speaker from the topic.

Many of us have a tendency to formulate an opinion about someone's point of view based on our history with that person or on our history with people who remind us of that person. These pre-conceived prejudices can be detrimental to a successful audit.

In the case of an internal audit, the auditor may have worked with the auditee in the past and formed opinions based on limited respect for him or her. In this situation it would be easy to tune out the auditee and miss learning of opportunities to improve the business that might have come out of the audit.

Perhaps the best example of this is an audit that I was observing for a client. It was apparent to me from the tension in the air that the internal auditor had a history with the auditee that prevented him from truly hearing everything that was being said. The auditee was leading the auditor to areas where improvement was needed, but the auditor would not follow up on these points.

Prior to leaving the work area, I stepped in to ask the auditee if we had missed anything—if there was anything that he would like to see added to the audit report to generate the attention it deserved. The auditee answered quietly and thoughtfully, saying that there were a couple of things that he would like to add. He had been trying to tell people for years that he could run the line 25-feet-a-minute faster than any other shift and produce at least 10 percent fewer defects. He thought he knew why, but couldn't get anyone to listen to him. Here was someone who actually wanted to share his expertise with the entire organization and no one would listen.

The bottom line is that we were able to quickly verify his claims through an analysis of readily available, electronically generated data. Because the auditee had followed all procedures, but ran the process in a different range of acceptable conditions, this was not considered an audit nonconformance. We cited an opportunity for improvement and provided the data to support it. As a result of this audit, the organization was able to calculate a return on this observation of more than $650,000 per year in increased productivity and decreased rework. Rising above preconceived prejudices to listen to employees who others are not hearing can be profitable for the organization.

Anticipating specific information.

An interesting facet of communication is that what we hear is often filtered by what we think we are about to hear. If you think you already know the answer to a question, you tend to hear that answer regardless of what the speaker is saying.

If an auditor knows too much about the process being audited, it may be difficult for him or her to hear the auditee. As strange as it sounds, I have witnessed this many times in the audits that I have observed. I have certainly been guilty of this myself. In helping clients implement the requirements of ISO 9001:2008, I will often help draft the quality manual and second-tier quality procedures. I will then return to the organization to train their internal auditors. As part of that training, I may conduct a mock audit for the class to illustrate what an audit might look like. Many times I have caught myself recording an answer before the auditee has had a chance to answer the question. Using auditors who are not responsible for the work being audited is critical to the success of an internal audit.

Thinking ahead.

The primary reason for failing to hear someone is the habit of "thinking ahead." When being introduced to someone for the first time, we may fail to hear his or her name because we are too busy thinking about what we might say to leave a great first impression. If we have a tendency to think ahead in everyday conversations, we will certainly have a tendency to think ahead during an audit.

As the auditee is speaking, he may mention something that you will want to follow up on. Trying to remember what you want to ask next will keep you from hearing what the auditee is currently saying.

One technique to prevent this from happening is to keep a blank sheet of paper in your lap during the audit. Let the note-taker take care of recording the facts observed during the audit. As the question-asker, you might write down just a key word or two that will remind you to follow up on important points. Having recorded the reminder, you are free to listen carefully to the rest of what the auditee is saying. This is common in the "branching" technique that is discussed later in this chapter.

Permitting environmental hindrance.

Often an internal audit will require that the auditor spend time in noisy or hot production areas. Having spent a large part of my career in the chemical industry along the Gulf Coast, I can tell you that some production areas are incredibly hot and very humid. If you are not acclimated to the heat and humidity, hearing what the auditee is saying will become more and more difficult as you become more miserable. In situations such as this, interview operations personnel for ten or fifteen minutes, then go inside and catch up on your notes. Repeat this pattern until you have solicited all the required information. Do not allow yourself to become so physically uncomfortable that you cannot truly listen to the auditee.

Being intimidated by complex technology.

When auditing a highly technical process, it is easy to tune out auditees who get into the technical aspects of their jobs. Nine times out of ten the auditee is simply speaking the accepted language. Independent of the process being audited, the auditor is not expected to know the technical aspects of a process. A thorough document review should allow you to know the technical language well enough at least to follow the conversation. Don't hesitate to ask the auditee to help you understand more clearly how the process works.

One time out of ten, however, the auditee will be trying to intimidate the auditor. When this happens, remember who is in control. If someone is trying to intimidate you, it is probably because he or she is intimidated by you. Handle these people as you would an insecure auditee and see if the situation improves. If not, remember that you knew before you began the audit what records you were going to review, how many, and what you would look for when you pulled them. Simply stick to the audit plan.

As you learn to optimize your audit skills, it's important to rise above these obstacles to listening.

EFFECTIVE USE OF THE CHECKLIST

As we discussed earlier, one drawback to a previously developed "backbone" checklist is the tendency for audits to become stale over the years. The auditor must remember that the checklist is intended to be a guide for the audit, not a script. The experienced auditor should not read from the checklist, but should lay down the checklist and talk with the auditee to learn everything possible about the process being audited.

If two auditors are conducting the audit, the note-taker should be the one to maintain the notes and data on the checklist. An experienced question-asker should not need to look at the checklist during the actual audit. Both auditors should have worked with the checklist enough during the preparation phase to have acquired a working knowledge of what is to be covered in the audit. The question-asker may then use either the branching technique or the tracing technique to learn everything possible about the process.

Branching Technique.

In the branching technique, the auditor begins the audit by asking the auditee to explain the process being audited. As the auditee is describing the process, the auditor is recording on a blank piece of paper key points that he or she would like to follow up on. When the auditee reaches the end of his or her train of thought, the auditor can begin at the first point and learn everything possible about that point, reviewing records along the way to verify conformance to ISO 9001:2008 and document procedures. An audit of a corrective action process, for example, might lead to the following key points being jotted down:

- Customer complaints

- Internal audits

- External audits

- Product or service nonconformance reports (NCRs)

- Corrective action log

- Root cause analysis

- Action plan

- Verification

- Close out

When the auditee has finished describing the corrective action process, the auditor can then go to the top of the list and ask questions and review records to fully understand each point. These questions will vary depending on where the audit leads. Examples of possible "branching" questions for each point are given below. (The points in parentheses are notes to the auditor rather than questions that the auditor might ask.)

- Customer complaints
  - Who typically receives customer complaints?
  - How are they recorded?
  - May I see that please?
  - Who has the authority to decide whether a Corrective Action Request (CAR) is warranted?
  - What action is taken if a CAR is not warranted? Is it recorded in some way? If so, may I see that please?
  - If a CAR is warranted, how is the CAR then generated? (Review complaints at random and ask the auditee to pull any indicated CARs. Hold on to them to review, as you get deeper into the CAR process.)
- Internal audits
  - How do you determine when a CAR is required following an internal audit?
  - Who has the authority to make that decision?
  - May I see the CARs that were generated following the last three audits? (Hold on to these CARs for review as you get deeper into the CAR process.)
- External audits
  - How is corrective action documented following an external audit?
  - Who is responsible for responding to the registrar (or customer, if there were any customer audits)?
  - May I see CARs that were generated following the last surveillance audit? (Hold on to these CARs to review as you get deeper into the CAR process.)
- Product or service NCRs (Nonconformance Reports)
  - How are product or service NCRs documented?
  - Who reviews them to determine the need for a CAR?
  - How is this evaluation made?
  - May I see CARs that have been generated in the past year to reduce nonconforming product? (Hold on to these CARs to review as you get deeper into the CAR process.)

- Corrective action log
  - You mentioned that you keep a corrective action log. May I see it please? (Review the log briefly to evaluate timeliness of corrective actions. If CARs were not pulled during the previous conversations, select CARs at random from the log to review.)

- Root cause analysis
  - Who is responsible for determining the root cause on the CAR?
  - Has there been any root cause analysis training for these people? (Review the identified cause on the CARs you have pulled in order to verify that the root cause of the problem was truly identified.)

- Action plan
  - (Review the CARs to determine whether the specified actions were sufficient to remove the root cause.)

- Verification
  - Who is responsible for verifying that corrective actions have indeed been implemented and that they were effective? (Review CARs to ensure that they include evidence that the actions taken were effective.)

- Close out
  - (Ensure that CARs were closed out without undue delay.)

When the question-asker has learned everything possible about the process, he or she turns to the note-taker and says, "Take it home. Have I missed anything or do you have anything else to add?" Where there are still blank spaces on the checklist, the note-taker follows up on those issues as well as other issues that came up during the audit that the question-asker did not explore.

TRACING TECHNIQUE

Another technique used in auditing is called tracing. Though this technique is more applicable to a full systems audit, it can be used in a process audit as long as the auditee stays within the stated scope. Using this technique, the auditor either starts at the beginning of a process and works all the way through to the end or begins at the end of the process and works backward. The typical example is to select one lot of a product and audit the entire quality management system as it relates to that one lot:

- Visually inspect the product if it is still at the facility. Is the product labeled and packaged in accordance with specified requirements?

- Is there any evidence of handling or storage damage?
- Was final product testing completed in accordance with specified requirements?
- Were final test results in compliance with specifications?
- Do records indicate the personnel responsible for its release?
- Was in-process testing completed per specified requirements?
- Were in-process test results within specification limits?
- Do records indicate the personnel responsible for in-process release?
- Were process parameters within acceptable limits while the product was being made?
- What lots of raw materials or component parts were used in this product?
- Was incoming inspection performed on that material in accordance with specified requirements?
- Were incoming inspection results within specified limits?
- Do records indicate the personnel responsible for their release?
- Were instruments used in incoming, in-process, and final product testing properly calibrated?

This example worked backward through a process. In a service industry, you may choose to take a service contract or project and work forward. This forward audit typically begins with the question, "Were customer requirements clearly defined for this project?" Then the auditor traces the project through each step to ensure that specified requirements were met.

Using one of these conversational styles of auditing is much more comfortable for the auditor and the auditee. New auditors will find that it is awkward to read questions off the checklist during the audit. After completing two or three audits, put the checklist down and start talking with the auditee. Not only is it more comfortable, but you will also learn a lot more during the audit. The auditee will tell you things you would have never dreamed to put in a checklist.

SAMPLING DATA

Throughout the audit, the auditor will review records to verify conformance to ISO 9001:2008 and to the organization's documented system as well as the effectiveness of the process being audited. As discussed in Chapter 5, determine the minimal sample size during the preparation phase of the audit and record it on the audit checklist.

During the audit, the auditor must ensure that representative samples are selected at random. In auditing a corrective action process, for example, the auditor may want to pull Corrective Action Requests (CAR) from each of the inputs into that process. These inputs may include:

- Internal audits

- External audits

- Customer complaints

- Product or service nonconformity reports

Within each representative category, pull the samples at random. Avoid the temptation to ask the auditee for an example of a CAR. The auditee will want to show you the very best example. If the auditee volunteers a sample, go ahead and audit it. Then pull 10 additional samples at random.

HANDLING DIFFICULT AUDITEES

If the proper environment has been adequately established, difficult auditees are rarely a problem during an internal audit. Occasionally auditors find themselves having to interview an auditee who simply resents or dislikes the audit process.

Most difficult auditees can be classified into one of four categories:

- The excessively nervous or anxious auditee

- The angry, resentful auditee

- The excessively proud auditee

- The auditee who is easily distracted by interruptions

We will discuss each of these categories and techniques to address each one.

The nervous, anxious auditee.

Techniques to put the nervous, anxious auditee at ease were discussed earlier in this chapter, so let's recap them:

- Simply restating and clarifying the purpose of the audit often goes a long way toward putting the auditee at ease.

- A few minutes of light conversation on a topic of interest to the auditee might help. In an internal audit, the auditor may know of a hobby the auditee enjoys or another topic of interest. If not, office pictures and wall decorations often make good conversation starters.

- As a last resort, the auditor and auditee can take a coffee break out of the work area. During the break, talk about the records that you will look at when the audit begins. Auditees who are prepared for what is expected will not feel that you are trying to trip them up.

- Sending the checklist to the auditees in advance is a good idea if there has been a history of nervous auditees in an area. Checklists should be based primarily on records and other facts and data. The auditor does not typically know in advance exactly which records will be reviewed, so the auditee cannot stage the audit using the checklist. The auditee must understand, however, that the checklist is simply a guide for the audit and will not be used as a script. The audit may go in other directions as the facts and data indicate. It does provide a general idea of what the auditors will be looking for. Sending the checklist in advance provides assurance that the auditor is not trying to trip up the auditees.

The angry, resentful auditee.

The angry, resentful auditee is not necessarily a detriment to the audit. If the auditor can discover what is causing the anger, he or she may be able to use the audit to address the concerns. Regardless of the cause of the anger, treating the auditee with dignity and respect will help to diffuse the situation. The auditor should find out, if possible, why the auditee is angry and then make every effort to use the audit to resolve the issue, if possible. Some of the more common responses are:

- "This ISO stuff is the most ridiculous thing this organization has ever done. It is just useless paperwork that keeps me from doing my job." As was discussed earlier, this is a wonderful opportunity to learn from the auditee where you can use the internal audit to improve the process—and perhaps to initiate significant improvement to the business as a whole. Explain to the auditee that ISO 9001 was never intended to weigh the organization down with excessive paperwork. Indeed, it is intended to streamline and optimize processes. Ask for help in finding ways that the audit can be used to improve the process and make it more efficient.

- "I have been in this place for twelve hours a day, seven days a week, for the past three months. Now you are here taking up another hour of my time. That means I stay tonight until 9:00 instead of my usual 8:00. What about this do you find difficult to understand?" Where there is anger there may be a legitimate reason for that anger.

To treat this auditee with respect is to use your audit time wisely. Explain the process. If that auditee can give you just five minutes and point you in the right direction, you will be happy to review the records on your own and get back with him in an hour or so to go over the results. The auditee may respond with, "Okay, you have your five minutes. Go." Good preparation will come in handy here. Or the auditee may say, "There is no way I would allow you to go through my records in my absence." In this case, tell him that you would actually prefer that he be there in case you have any questions. You were just trying to save him some time. Treating this auditee's time with respect will cause him to return just enough respect to provide the information you need.

Make it a goal to find opportunities to streamline this process to save this auditee time in his day. You have an opportunity to create a real champion for the audit process.

- "We've jumped through every quality hoop there is. If it has three or four letters, we've done it! TQM. APQP. FMEA. SPC. And now ISO. Why can't we just do our jobs?" The auditor should be armed with specific, tangible improvements that have been generated through the implementation of ISO 9001 or through the internal audit process. First, get the basics out of the way: "You really are right! But good, bad, or indifferent, we must keep our ISO 9001 registration if we want to do business with our biggest customers. No ISO, no business. But having said that, ISO really has done some pretty good things for us..." Then talk about some of the successes that affect the auditee. Stress that you can either play games with the audit, or actually use it to try to make things better.

If auditees will not verbalize their frustrations, it is possible that they may simply be nervous about the audit. Treat them as you would any nervous auditee and see whether that helps alleviate the tension.

The excessively proud auditee.

The excessively proud auditee is perhaps the most difficult to handle in the internal audit. This auditee may have worked nights and weekends to implement processes that he or she is truly proud of. No one else has even noticed. And now here you are to look at everything they have done! They may be truly excited about showing you everything they have accomplished.

To help understand the perspective of this auditee, remember the last time you redecorated your kitchen or bathroom yourself. (Contracting the work doesn't count.) God bless any visitor to your home! How excited were you to open and close cabinets, flush toilets, turn on faucets? How would you have felt if your friends and family had responded to this demonstration with, "You missed a spot here. Why did you put this cabinet in such an inconvenient place? Have you noticed that this row of tiles is a little crooked?" We frequently do this when we audit.

The first step in dealing with the proud auditee is to spend that first five minutes or so complimenting the work they have done. They may be proud because they have a right to be proud. Give them the recognition they need and deserve.

Then pull out the checklist. This is the only audit for which I recommend that you read directly off the checklist in order to maintain focus and order. Avoid words such as "discrepancy," "failure," and "nonconformance" unless you want to see tears. Report findings in a way that would be perceived as adding extra value to a great process. Only once in 27 years of auditing have I discovered a substandard process while auditing a genuinely proud auditee. Typically, these guys have worked hard and deserve a sincere "nice job."

The easily distracted auditee.

Handling the easily distracted auditee is not complicated. Get the auditee away from the most common distraction: a ringing telephone. Invite him or her to a conference room—without the BlackBerry or cell phone—to finish the audit. If the auditee is expecting an important call, ask him to forward his calls to an associate who can come get him if the call comes through.

Difficult auditees are not the norm. If the appropriate environment has been established, most auditees are quite helpful. Some have even been appreciative of the hard work performed by the auditor!

After the data-gathering phase of the audit is complete, the auditors must analyze that data, prepare an effective report, and conduct a closing meeting. These activities are addressed in Chapter 7.

7

Reporting the Audit

Once data has been gathered, you will analyze the data to determine what will be classified as audit nonconformances, audit observations, and opportunities for improvement. As discussed in Chapter 4, the auditor is not responsible for ensuring timely, thorough corrective action following an audit. That is the responsibility of the auditee's management or process owner, who is in the best position to know what corrective action will be most effective.

How the auditor reports the findings, however, can either encourage or hinder timely, thorough corrective action. In this chapter, we will discuss how to classify audit findings, how to write effective Corrective Action Requests, how to document the audit report, and how to conduct an effective closing meeting.

TYPES OF AUDIT FINDINGS

Though each organization uses its own terminology, most have three general types of audit findings. For the sake of this discussion, I will define the terms that will be used in this chapter:

- A *nonconformance* is the breakdown, or partial breakdown, of a process in the quality management system. An audit nonconformance typically requires root cause analysis, root cause elimination, and/or a change in how the process is to be performed. As such, it requires a Corrective Action Request (or your organization's equivalent) to document the action taken. Registrars often call this type of finding a major nonconformance, or a systemic finding.

  Examples of nonconformance may include:
  - Of the 10 CAR's reviewed, only one showed evidence that the action taken was implemented and effective.

– There is no formal process to evaluate or re-evaluate suppliers of raw materials or component parts.

– Of the 10 pieces of equipment audited for compliance to the company's preventive maintenance (PM) requirements, eight were three months or more past due on those required PM activities.

– Management review records do not show evidence that any action items were identified during the review to result in continual improvement of the quality management system or its related processes, products, and services.

• An *observation* is a minor deviation from an otherwise well-implemented process. It is typically due to a minor oversight on the part of the auditee and it is unlikely to result in nonconforming product or service. Root cause analysis is rarely required for observations; a CAR is not typically warranted. Observations may be recorded on an Audit Action Item List (see Appendix D) to facilitate the analysis of trends. When multiple observations of a similar nature are noted during the audit or detected on the Audit Action Item List, the auditor or management representative may choose to initiate a CAR and treat the trend as a nonconformance. Registrars may refer to this type of finding as an observation or an isolated finding.

Examples of observations include:

– Of the ten training records reviewed, one was not signed by the instructor.

– Of the three identified action items reviewed from the past management review meeting, one was not updated on the Action Item Log to show that it had been completed.

– Two of ten auditees interviewed were not completely aware of the organization's objectives and how their activities affect our ability to meet those objectives.

– Though all five of the corrective actions reviewed from internal audits were thoroughly completed and verified as having been effective, two were not completed by the required completion date.

• An *opportunity for improvement* is a finding based on facts and data that indicates a potential improvement opportunity. Action is not required for an opportunity for improvement. However, the auditor should include as much supporting data as possible to encourage action.

Internal auditors often struggle over the decision to classify a finding as a nonconformance or an observation. A good rule of thumb is this: If the finding requires the analysis and/or elimination of a root cause or if it requires a change to the current process, it is typically a nonconformance; a CAR should be initiated. If root cause analysis is not indicated, the finding is probably an observation. Observations should still be recorded on some type of Audit Action Item List, however, so that repetitive observations of a similar nature can be easily identified. Repetitive observations may indicate that the process is breaking down and a CAR may be required.

WRITING EFFECTIVE CARs

When a CAR is indicated by the audit findings, the auditor typically has the responsibility to initiate it. In some organizations, however, the management representative is responsible for reviewing audit findings and generating the CAR. Regardless of who initiates it, it must contain vital information to encourage timely, thorough corrective action.

An example of a CAR form is provided in Appendix D and on the enclosed CD to facilitate your customization. The auditor is responsible for completing the CAR down through a description of the problem. If during the audit a probable root cause was discovered, the auditor may choose to record that on the CAR as well. The description of the problem must include two things if the auditee is to respond in a positive manner. It must include (1) a reference to ISO 9001:2008 or the organization's own documentation and (2) objective evidence to support the finding. If the location of the finding will help focus the corrective action in the right place, the auditor should provide that information as well.

The following examples of problem statements are poorly written:

- Employees do not seem to understand the policy statement or the organization's objectives. (Ref: 5.3 and 5.4.1)

- Document control of customer specifications needs a lot of improvement. (Ref: 4.2.3)

- Operators in the "B" unit are not running the process in accordance with the appropriate batch sheet. (Ref: 7.5)

- No one is reviewing customer satisfaction data. (Ref: 8.2.1)

- Nonconforming product is often not identified. (Ref: 8.3)

In each of these examples, references to the standard are vague and there is no objective evidence to support the finding. The following examples include more specific references and the supporting objective evidence:

- Of the 10 employees interviewed, only five were familiar with our quality policy statement (Ref: 5.3.d) and only three were familiar with our quality objectives and how their activities affect our ability to meet those objectives. (Ref: 6.2.2.d)

- Of the five customer specifications reviewed in the QC Lab, three were at least one revision out of date and none were approved by the Customer Manager as required in BP-01. (Ref: 4.2.3.a/d)

- Of the five batch sheets reviewed in the "B" unit, all five showed the temperatures and pressures to be running outside the acceptable limits specified on the batch sheet. (Ref: 7.5.1.e) Auditor's note: Auditees suggested that the batch sheets were not revised after the last process improvement team implemented changes to the process.

- There is no defined process to review customer satisfaction data and initiate CARs where indicated. Responsibilities relative to this review have not been defined. (Ref: 8.2.1/8.4/8.5.1/5.5.1)

- During the audit, three rejected products were noted on the "D" line that were not identified or segregated. (Ref: 8.3 and BP-13, Section 5.4)

If the auditor is able to identify specific examples where these issues have caused nonconforming product to be shipped, premium freight to be paid, or other added costs to be incurred, this additional information should be recorded on the CAR and presented at the closing meeting. For example:

- Of the five customer specifications reviewed in the QC Lab, three were at least one revision out of date and none were approved by the Customer Manager as required in BP-01. (Ref: 4.2.3.a/d)

  Auditor's note: Of the last three shipments returned from the customer, two were caused by obsolete specifications.

- There is no defined process to review customer satisfaction data and initiate CARs where indicated. Responsibilities relative to this review have not been defined. (Ref: 8.2.1/8.4/8.5.1/5.5.1)

  Auditor's note: There are two specific areas that have been rated very low in the last two annual customer surveys: on-time delivery and customer service. We have lost at least two customers in the last six months due to these issues.

- During the audit, three rejected products were noted on the "D" line that were not identified or segregated. (Ref: 8.3 and BP-13, Section 5.4)

  Auditor's note: Three customer complaints were noted in the past six months because we shipped product that had already been found to be reject.

Adding clear evidence indicating that a resolution of these issues will result in a return on investment will increase the probability of timely, thorough corrective action. Identification of the samples observed are available in the completed audit checklist, which should be maintained as part of the audit record. Including the sample identifications in the CAR encourages the auditee to "fix" the samples instead of correcting the process.

THE AUDIT REPORT

The audit report should include a summary page describing the key information related to the audit. The summary page should include:

- Names of the auditors

- Date(s) of the audit

- Scope of the audit—including the process(es) audited with the applicable reference to ISO 9001:2008 and the areas or departments visited during the audit

- Summary of nonconformances

- Observations noted

- Opportunities for improvement

- Examples of outstanding performance or evidence of improvement since the last audit

- Expectations for corrective action responses

An example of an Audit Summary Report form can be found in Appendix D and on the enclosed CD to facilitate your customization.

The auditor can then attach copies of the initiated CARs and the Audit Action Item List to the Audit Summary to complete the audit report. The key is to provide the required information to the appropriate managers in a format that enables the report to be issued in a reasonable timeframe. To encourage timely corrective action, the report should be issued within 24 hours of the audit and should be distributed at or before the closing meeting.

When audit reports are issued two weeks or longer after the audit, they typically end up in a manager's "to-do" pile as a reminder to ask clarifying questions about the audit. A manager who does not understand why something was a finding or who does not understand the evidence to support a finding isn't likely to follow up with questions. One thing most people's "to-do" piles have in common is that they rarely get done.

THE CLOSING MEETING

The closing meeting, with at least the managers from the areas audited or process owners, should be conducted within 24 hours of the audit. The purpose of the closing meeting is to ensure that those responsible for corrective action understand what the findings are, why they are findings, and what type of corrective action is required.

The audit report should be issued at the closing meeting and those in attendance should be given the opportunity to question and understand each finding in the report. If a manager leaves that meeting doubting the validity of a finding, timely corrective action probably will not occur.

If the auditors were able to uncover facts and data to support significant returns on investment (ROI) based on the indicated corrective action, that information should be provided at the closing meeting. It is rare that complete ROI data will be available in that timeframe, but any information leading to the calculation of returns should be provided to encourage those managers in attendance to take timely corrective action.

SUMMARY OF AUDIT REPORTING

Though auditors do not have responsibility for corrective action following an internal audit, there are four things they can do to encourage such activity:

- Ensure that Corrective Action Requests contain the reference for the finding and specific objective evidence

- Issue the audit report within 24 hours

- Conduct a closing meeting with at least the manager(s) of the area(s) included in the audit

- Provide information relating to ROI on the indicated corrective action if that information is available

By following these suggestions, the auditors will ensure that they have done everything within their power to facilitate timely, thorough corrective action following an internal audit.

8

Follow-Up Audit Activities

ISO 9001:2008 requires that follow-up activities take place after the audit to ensure that corrective action taken was implemented and was effective at resolving the audit finding. Organizations typically are good at verifying that corrective action was implemented, but weak on verifying the effectiveness of that action.

The best individual to verify the effectiveness of the corrective action taken is one of the original auditors who recorded the finding. The auditors saw the process as it was before the audit and are in a good position to evaluate the effectiveness of the corrective action.

Perhaps the best way to evaluate the effectiveness of corrective actions is to provide examples of what is acceptable and what is not for specific audit findings.

FINDING:

"Of the 10 employees interviewed, only five were familiar with our quality policy statement (Ref: 5.3.d) and only three were familiar with our quality objectives and how their activities affect our ability to meet those objectives. (Ref: 6.2.2.d)"

The corrective action defined for this finding required the organization to provide additional training for all of its employees in order to ensure that each understood the policy statement, the supporting objectives, and how their specific activities affected the organization's ability to achieve the policy and the objectives. Given this defined action plan, many auditors verify the corrective action by reviewing training records for a sample of employees at random and verifying that they had the required training. Such verification ensures that corrective action was taken, but falls short of verifying that the action taken was effective.

The only way to verify the effectiveness of the action taken is to re-audit this portion of the quality management system. Do the results indicate that the training provided was effective? This may involve questioning 10 to 20 employees at random throughout the organization to verify that they are now aware of the policy and the objectives and of how their specific activities affect the organization's ability to achieve both. The results of this re-audit should be recorded in the verification section of the CAR.

FINDING:

"Of the five customer specifications reviewed in the QC Lab, three were at least one revision out of date and none were approved by the Customer Manager as required in BP-01. (Ref: 4.2.3.a/d)"

In this case, the cause of the problem was determined to be that the facility audited was not on the corporate Customer Service Department distribution list for customer specifications. Consequently, the specifications were not being updated at this facility.

A superficial re-audit of this finding would verify that the five customer specifications have now been updated and are properly approved. This verification activity does not even fully verify that adequate corrective action was *taken*, much less that the corrective action was *effective*.

A slightly better approach would be to verify that the distribution list in the Customer Service Department had been updated to include this particular facility and that that all customer specifications in the Lab had been updated. Still, this activity only verifies that the corrective action was taken, but supplies no evidence to support that the action was effective.

To verify the effectiveness of the action taken, the auditor should allow the new process to be implemented on several specification revisions. The auditor can then identify the last three to five spec changes from the Customer Service Department and verify that all appropriate copies in the facility were properly approved and issued. This data should then be recorded in the verification section of the CAR.

FINDING:

"Of the five batch sheets reviewed in the 'B' unit, all five showed the temperatures and pressures to be running outside the acceptable limits specified on the batch sheet. (Ref: 7.5.1.e) Auditor's note: Auditees suggested that the batch sheets were not revised after the last process improvement team recommended changes to the process."

The cause of the finding in this case was determined to be that the quality improvement process used at this facility did not include the updating of applicable documentation when changes to the process are made. The organization updated its quality improvement process to include this step before the team disbanded.

A superficial verification of this audit finding would be to verify that the quality improvement process had indeed been updated and that batch sheets had been revised to reflect current operating conditions. Again, such verification would prove that corrective action has been taken and that the current batch sheets were correct, but would not ensure that the quality improvement process has been effectively implemented to provide adequate documentation for future process changes.

The auditor should do the verification described above, but should also allow enough time to pass so that several quality improvement teams can complete their assigned tasks. The auditor should then verify that any changes recommended by the team resulted in appropriate documentation revisions to reflect those changes.

> **FINDING:**
>
> *"There is no defined process to review customer satisfaction data and initiate CARs where indicated. Responsibilities relative to this review have not been defined. (Ref: 8.2.1/8.4/8.5.1/5.5.1)"*

As a result of this audit finding, the organization updated its customer satisfaction procedure to include responsibility for reviewing the data to determine the need for corrective or preventive action, how that review should be conducted, and how the CAR or PAR should be initiated.

To effectively verify this action, the auditor should ensure that the procedure had indeed been revised and appropriately issued. He or she should then re-audit the next customer survey results to ensure that the data was reviewed as documented and that action was taken where indicated by the data.

> **FINDING:**
>
> *"During the audit, three rejected products were noted on the 'D' line that were not identified or segregated. (Ref: 8.3 and BP-13, Section 5.4)"*

In this case, the organization found that the procedure for the control of nonconforming products was well written, but was not being followed. The root cause was found to be that employees were not aware of what the procedure required. The corrective action included not only training employees on the current procedure for the control of nonconforming products, but also updating the document control procedure so that appropriate personnel are made aware of the changes and adequate training is provided where required.

To verify the effectiveness of this CAR, the auditor should indeed re-audit the control of nonconforming product to ensure that reject products were now being identified and segregated per the procedure. But the auditor should also find out whether the document control procedure has been updated and properly issued to specify how procedural changes will be communicated to appropriate personnel and how and when appropriate training is provided. The auditor should then review recent document changes to ensure that the new process is being followed.

Each of these examples illustrates that the auditor must go beyond verifying that the symptoms have been fixed. The auditor must ensure that the process has been changed so that similar process breakdowns are not likely to occur in the future.

SUMMARY OF EFFECTIVE INTERNAL AUDITING

This book was intended to provide specific tools and techniques to facilitate internal audits that are effective at improving the business and its bottom line. The key points in such an effective audit process include:

- Establishing an environment where managers and employees value the internal audit as a critical tool in its overall quality improvement strategy.

- Focusing on the successes of an internal audit—not just the number of findings.

- Finding ways to communicate those successes throughout the organization so that managers and employees are aware of the benefits that have been derived from the internal audit process.

- If possible, calculating the return on investment for corrective actions taken as a result of internal audits and communicating these successes throughout the organization.

- Ensuring that auditors adequately prepare so that they will know before they conduct the audit how effectiveness of the process will be evaluated, what records will be pulled, how many will be pulled, and what will be reviewed.

- Ensuring that auditors are trained to verify that desired outputs of the processes are clearly defined and that inputs to the process are provided to ensure that the process can achieve the desired outputs.

- Issuing the audit report within 24 hours of the audit.

- Ensuring that any CARs initiated as a result of the audit contain an appropriate reference to the standard or the organization's own documented procedures as well as clear objective evidence.

- Conducting a closing meeting with all applicable managers or process owners to ensure that issues in the report are clearly understood.

- Thoroughly verifying that any required corrective actions have been effectively completed before closing them out.

It is sincerely my desire that these tools and techniques will help you to improve the effectiveness of your internal audit process and achieve measurable benefits for your organization and its bottom line.

Appendix A
Sample Process Models

Process

- Acme Process Map
- Calibration Process Model
- Corrective Action Process Model
- Customer Satisfaction Process Model
- Design Control Process Model
- Inspection Process Model
- Internal Audit Process Model
- Maintenance Process Model
- Management Review Process Model
- Order Entry Process Model
- Preventive Action Process Model
- Production Process Model
- Purchasing Process Model
- Shipping Process Model

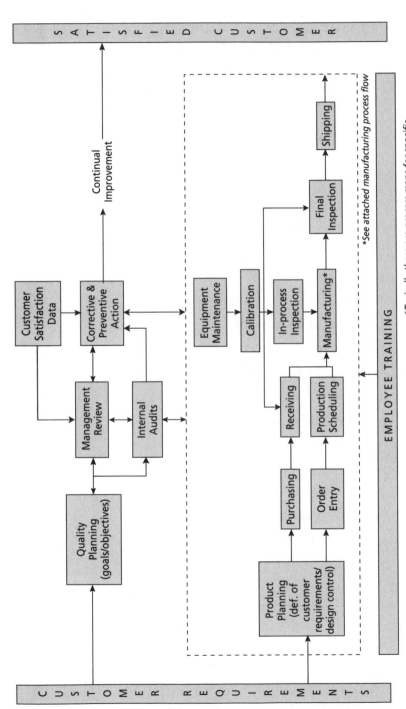

Appendix A Acme process map.

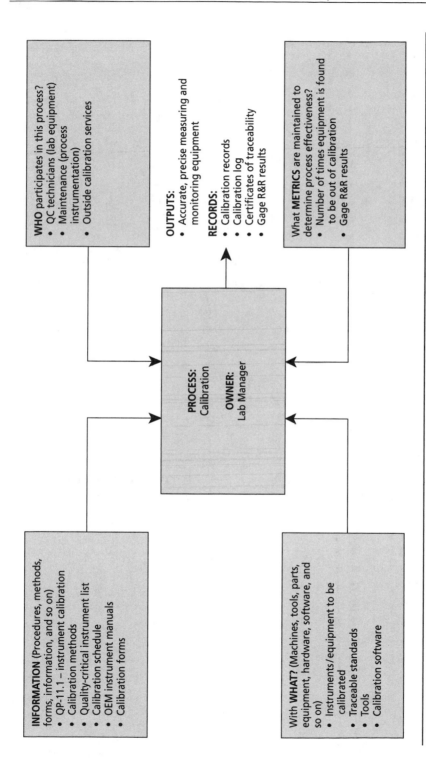

INFORMATION (Procedures, methods, forms, information, and so on)
- QP-11.1 – instrument calibration
- Calibration methods
- Quality-critical instrument list
- Calibration schedule
- OEM instrument manuals
- Calibration forms

WHO participates in this process?
- QC technicians (lab equipment)
- Maintenance (process instrumentation)
- Outside calibration services

PROCESS:
Calibration

OWNER:
Lab Manager

OUTPUTS:
- Accurate, precise measuring and monitoring equipment

RECORDS:
- Calibration records
- Calibration log
- Certificates of traceability
- Gage R&R results

With **WHAT?** (Machines, tools, parts, equipment, hardware, software, and so on)
- Instruments/equipment to be calibrated
- Traceable standards
- Tools
- Calibration software

What **METRICS** are maintained to determine process effectiveness?
- Number of times equipment is found to be out of calibration
- Gage R&R results

Appendix A Calibration process model.

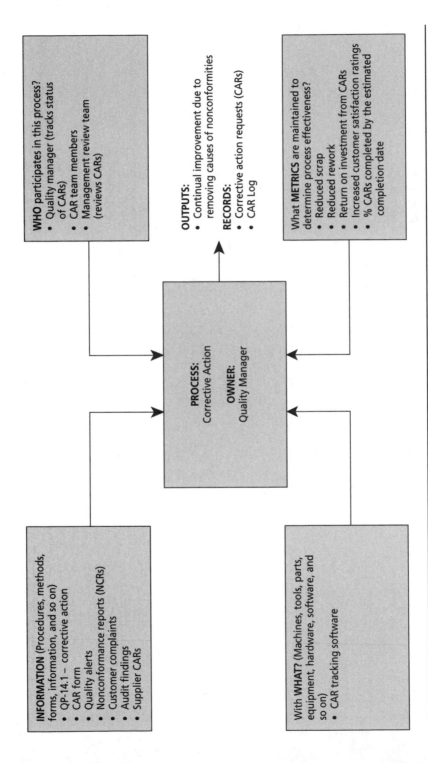

WHO participates in this process?
- Quality manager (tracks status of CARs)
- CAR team members
- Management review team (reviews CARs)

OUTPUTS:
- Continual improvement due to removing causes of nonconformities

RECORDS:
- Corrective action requests (CARs)
- CAR Log

What **METRICS** are maintained to determine process effectiveness?
- Reduced scrap
- Reduced rework
- Return on investment from CARs
- Increased customer satisfaction ratings
- % CARs completed by the estimated completion date

PROCESS:
Corrective Action

OWNER:
Quality Manager

INFORMATION (Procedures, methods, forms, information, and so on)
- QP-14.1 – corrective action
- CAR form
- Quality alerts
- Nonconformance reports (NCRs)
- Customer complaints
- Audit findings
- Supplier CARs

With **WHAT?** (Machines, tools, parts, equipment, hardware, software, and so on)
- CAR tracking software

Appendix A   Corrective action process model.

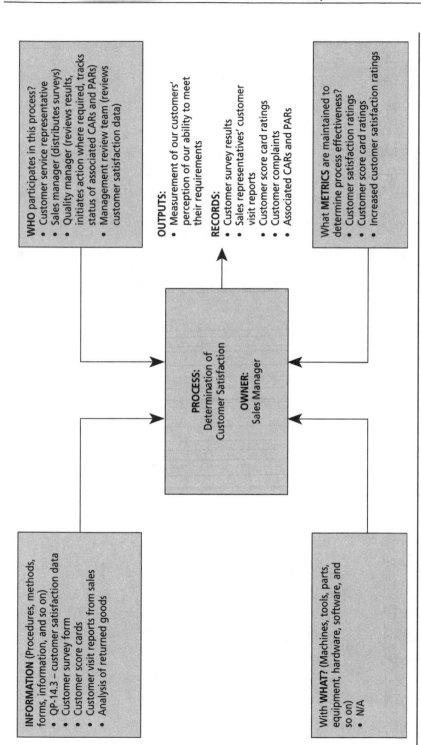

WHO participates in this process?
- Customer service representative
- Sales manager (distributes surveys)
- Quality manager (reviews results, initiates action where required, tracks status of associated CARs and PARs)
- Management review team (reviews customer satisfaction data)

OUTPUTS:
- Measurement of our customers' perception of our ability to meet their requirements

RECORDS:
- Customer survey results
- Sales representatives' customer visit reports
- Customer score card ratings
- Customer complaints
- Associated CARs and PARs

What **METRICS** are maintained to determine process effectiveness?
- Customer satisfaction ratings
- Customer score card ratings
- Increased customer satisfaction ratings

PROCESS:
Determination of
Customer Satisfaction

OWNER:
Sales Manager

INFORMATION (Procedures, methods, forms, information, and so on)
- QP-14.3 – customer satisfaction data
- Customer survey form
- Customer score cards
- Customer visit reports from sales
- Analysis of returned goods

With **WHAT?** (Machines, tools, parts, equipment, hardware, software, and so on)
- N/A

Appendix A Customer satisfaction process model.

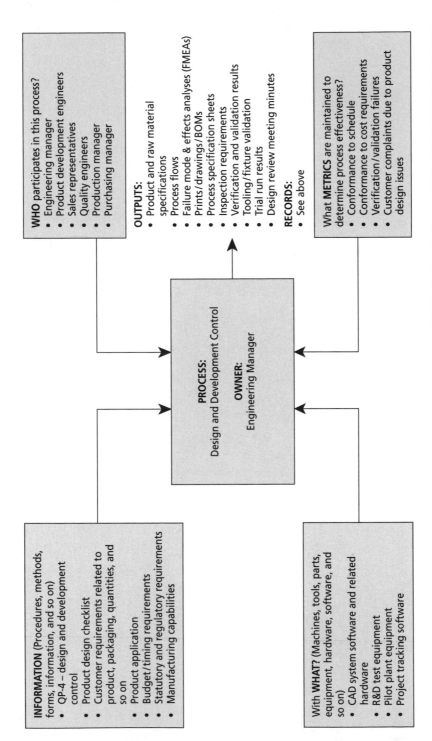

WHO participates in this process?
- Engineering manager
- Product development engineers
- Sales representatives
- Quality engineers
- Production manager
- Purchasing manager

OUTPUTS:
- Product and raw material specifications
- Process flows
- Failure mode & effects analyses (FMEAs)
- Prints/drawings/BOMs
- Process specification sheets
- Inspection requirements
- Verification and validation results
- Tooling/fixture validation
- Trial run results
- Design review meeting minutes

RECORDS:
- See above

What **METRICS** are maintained to determine process effectiveness?
- Conformance to schedule
- Conformance to cost requirements
- Verification/validation failures
- Customer complaints due to product design issues

PROCESS:
Design and Development Control

OWNER:
Engineering Manager

INFORMATION (Procedures, methods, forms, information, and so on)
- QP-4 – design and development control
- Product design checklist
- Customer requirements related to product, packaging, quantities, and so on
- Product application
- Budget/timing requirements
- Statutory and regulatory requirements
- Manufacturing capabilities

With **WHAT?** (Machines, tools, parts, equipment, hardware, software, and so on)
- CAD system software and related hardware
- R&D test equipment
- Pilot plant equipment
- Project tracking software

Appendix A   Design control process model.

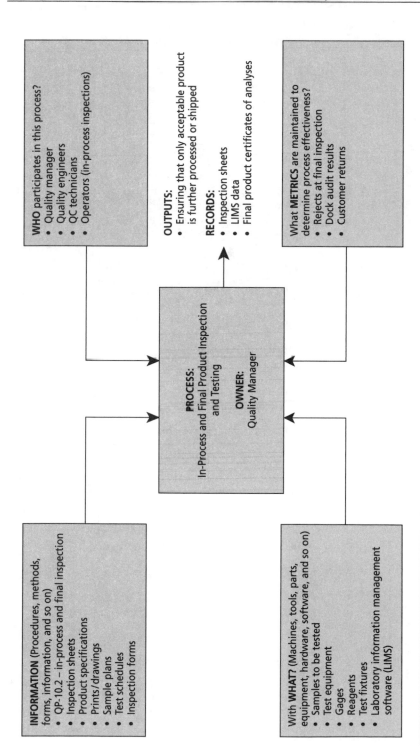

WHO participates in this process?
- Quality manager
- Quality engineers
- QC technicians
- Operators (in-process inspections)

INFORMATION (Procedures, methods, forms, information, and so on)
- QP-10.2 – in-process and final inspection
- Inspection sheets
- Product specifications
- Prints/drawings
- Sample plans
- Test schedules
- Inspection forms

PROCESS:
In-Process and Final Product Inspection and Testing

OWNER:
Quality Manager

OUTPUTS:
- Ensuring that only acceptable product is further processed or shipped

RECORDS:
- Inspection sheets
- LIMS data
- Final product certificates of analyses

What **METRICS** are maintained to determine process effectiveness?
- Rejects at final inspection
- Dock audit results
- Customer returns

With **WHAT?** (Machines, tools, parts, equipment, hardware, software, and so on)
- Samples to be tested
- Test equipment
- Gages
- Reagents
- Test fixtures
- Laboratory information management software (LIMS)

Appendix A   Inspection process model.

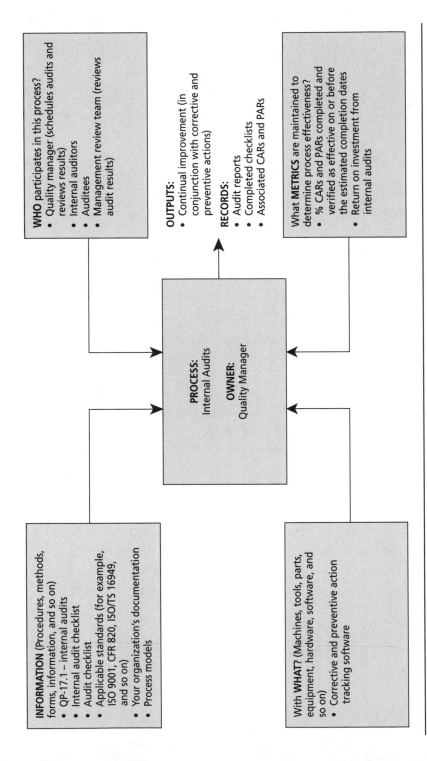

WHO participates in this process?
- Quality manager (schedules audits and reviews results)
- Internal auditors
- Auditees
- Management review team (reviews audit results)

OUTPUTS:
- Continual improvement (in conjunction with corrective and preventive actions)

RECORDS:
- Audit reports
- Completed checklists
- Associated CARs and PARs

What **METRICS** are maintained to determine process effectiveness?
- % CARs and PARs completed and verified as effective on or before the estimated completion dates
- Return on investment from internal audits

PROCESS:
Internal Audits

OWNER:
Quality Manager

INFORMATION (Procedures, methods, forms, information, and so on)
- QP-17.1 – internal audits
- Internal audit checklist
- Audit checklist
- Applicable standards (for example, ISO 9001, CFR 820, ISO/TS 16949, and so on)
- Your organization's documentation
- Process models

With **WHAT?** (Machines, tools, parts, equipment, hardware, software, and so on)
- Corrective and preventive action tracking software

Appendix A   Internal audit process model.

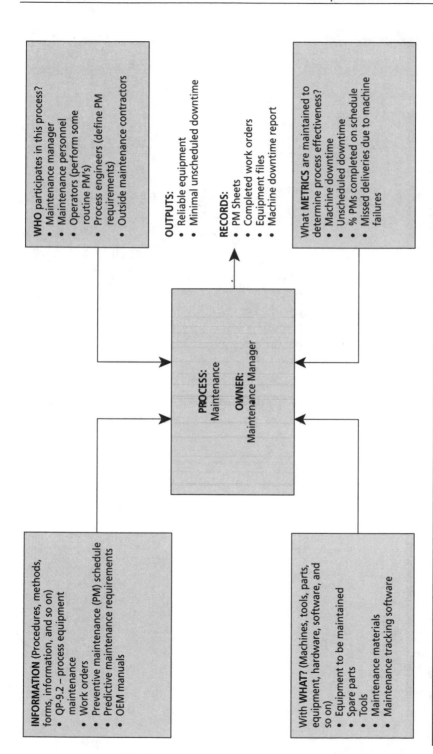

WHO participates in this process?
- Maintenance manager
- Maintenance personnel
- Operators (perform some routine PM's)
- Process engineers (define PM requirements)
- Outside maintenance contractors

OUTPUTS:
- Reliable equipment
- Minimal unscheduled downtime

RECORDS:
- PM Sheets
- Completed work orders
- Equipment files
- Machine downtime report

What **METRICS** are maintained to determine process effectiveness?
- Machine downtime
- Unscheduled downtime
- % PMs completed on schedule
- Missed deliveries due to machine failures

PROCESS:
Maintenance

OWNER:
Maintenance Manager

INFORMATION (Procedures, methods, forms, information, and so on)
- QP-9.2 – process equipment maintenance
- Work orders
- Preventive maintenance (PM) schedule
- Predictive maintenance requirements
- OEM manuals

With **WHAT?** (Machines, tools, parts, equipment, hardware, software, and so on)
- Equipment to be maintained
- Spare parts
- Tools
- Maintenance materials
- Maintenance tracking software

Appendix A   Maintenance process model.

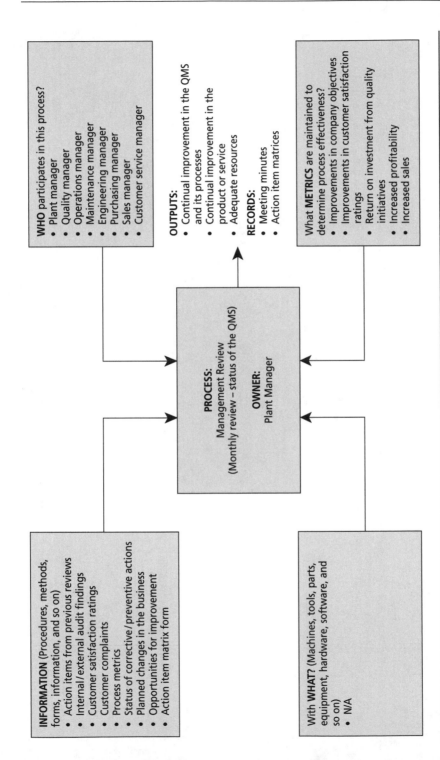

WHO participates in this process?
- Plant manager
- Quality manager
- Operations manager
- Maintenance manager
- Engineering manager
- Purchasing manager
- Sales manager
- Customer service manager

OUTPUTS:
- Continual improvement in the QMS and its processes
- Continual improvement in the product or service
- Adequate resources

RECORDS:
- Meeting minutes
- Action item matrices

What **METRICS** are maintained to determine process effectiveness?
- Improvements in company objectives
- Improvements in customer satisfaction ratings
- Return on investment from quality initiatives
- Increased profitability
- Increased sales

PROCESS:
Management Review
(Monthly review – status of the QMS)

OWNER:
Plant Manager

INFORMATION (Procedures, methods, forms, information, and so on)
- Action items from previous reviews
- Internal/external audit findings
- Customer satisfaction ratings
- Customer complaints
- Process metrics
- Status of corrective/preventive actions
- Planned changes in the business
- Opportunities for improvement
- Action item matrix form

With **WHAT?** (Machines, tools, parts, equipment, hardware, software, and so on)
- N/A

Appendix A Management review process model.

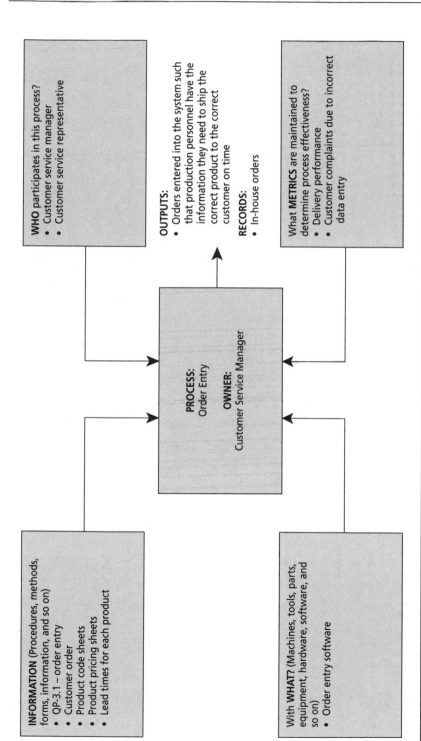

WHO participates in this process?
- Customer service manager
- Customer service representative

OUTPUTS:
- Orders entered into the system such that production personnel have the information they need to ship the correct product to the correct customer on time

RECORDS:
- In-house orders

What **METRICS** are maintained to determine process effectiveness?
- Delivery performance
- Customer complaints due to incorrect data entry

PROCESS:
Order Entry

OWNER:
Customer Service Manager

INFORMATION (Procedures, methods, forms, information, and so on)
- QP-3.1 – order entry
- Customer order
- Product code sheets
- Product pricing sheets
- Lead times for each product

With **WHAT?** (Machines, tools, parts, equipment, hardware, software, and so on)
- Order entry software

Appendix A   Order entry process model.

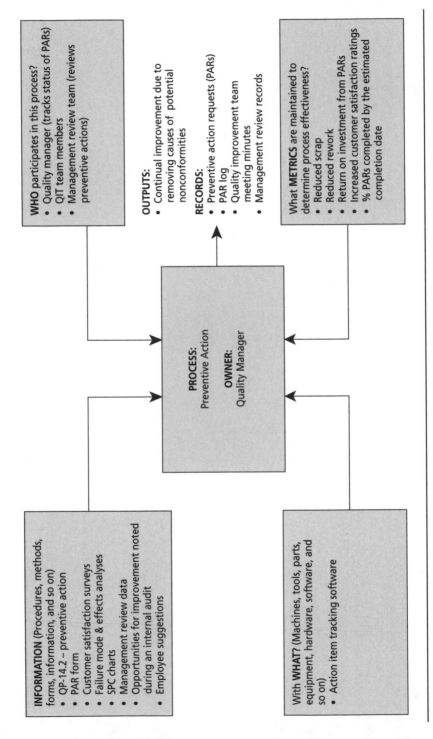

WHO participates in this process?
- Quality manager (tracks status of PARs)
- QIT team members
- Management review team (reviews preventive actions)

OUTPUTS:
- Continual improvement due to removing causes of potential nonconformities

RECORDS:
- Preventive action requests (PARs)
- PAR log
- Quality improvement team meeting minutes
- Management review records

What **METRICS** are maintained to determine process effectiveness?
- Reduced scrap
- Reduced rework
- Return on investment from PARs
- Increased customer satisfaction ratings
- % PARs completed by the estimated completion date

PROCESS:
Preventive Action

OWNER:
Quality Manager

INFORMATION (Procedures, methods, forms, information, and so on)
- QP-14.2 – preventive action
- PAR form
- Customer satisfaction surveys
- Failure mode & effects analyses
- SPC charts
- Management review data
- Opportunities for improvement noted during an internal audit
- Employee suggestions

With **WHAT?** (Machines, tools, parts, equipment, hardware, software, and so on)
- Action item tracking software

Appendix A   Preventive action process model.

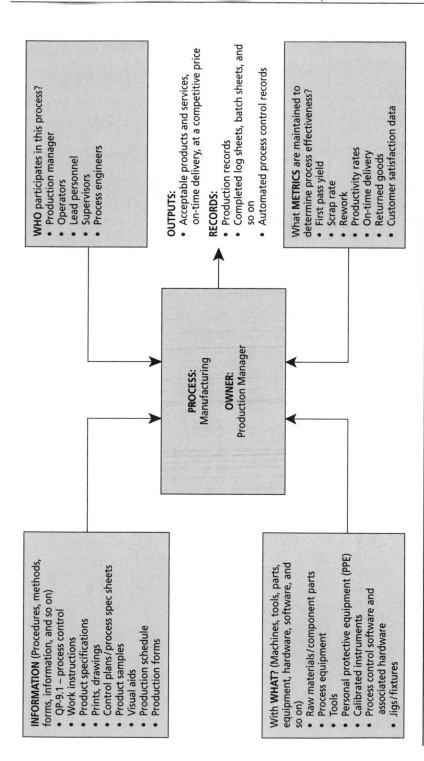

WHO participates in this process?
- Production manager
- Operators
- Lead personnel
- Supervisors
- Process engineers

OUTPUTS:
- Acceptable products and services, on-time delivery, at a competitive price

RECORDS:
- Production records
- Completed log sheets, batch sheets, and so on
- Automated process control records

What **METRICS** are maintained to determine process effectiveness?
- First pass yield
- Scrap rate
- Rework
- Productivity rates
- On-time delivery
- Returned goods
- Customer satisfaction data

PROCESS:
Manufacturing

OWNER:
Production Manager

INFORMATION (Procedures, methods, forms, information, and so on)
- QP-9.1 – process control
- Work instructions
- Product specifications
- Prints, drawings
- Control plans/process spec sheets
- Product samples
- Visual aids
- Production schedule
- Production forms

With **WHAT?** (Machines, tools, parts, equipment, hardware, software, and so on)
- Raw materials/component parts
- Process equipment
- Tools
- Personal protective equipment (PPE)
- Calibrated instruments
- Process control software and associated hardware
- Jigs/fixtures

Appendix A Production process model.

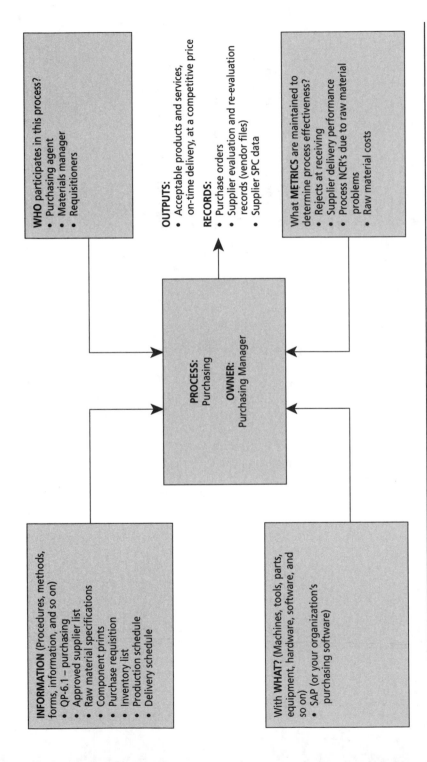

WHO participates in this process?
- Purchasing agent
- Materials manager
- Requisitioners

OUTPUTS:
- Acceptable products and services, on-time delivery, at a competitive price

RECORDS:
- Purchase orders
- Supplier evaluation and re-evaluation records (vendor files)
- Supplier SPC data

What **METRICS** are maintained to determine process effectiveness?
- Rejects at receiving
- Supplier delivery performance
- Process NCR's due to raw material problems
- Raw material costs

PROCESS:
Purchasing

OWNER:
Purchasing Manager

INFORMATION (Procedures, methods, forms, information, and so on)
- QP-6.1 – purchasing
- Approved supplier list
- Raw material specifications
- Component prints
- Purchase requisition
- Inventory list
- Production schedule
- Delivery schedule

With **WHAT?** (Machines, tools, parts, equipment, hardware, software, and so on)
- SAP (or your organization's purchasing software)

Appendix A Purchasing process model.

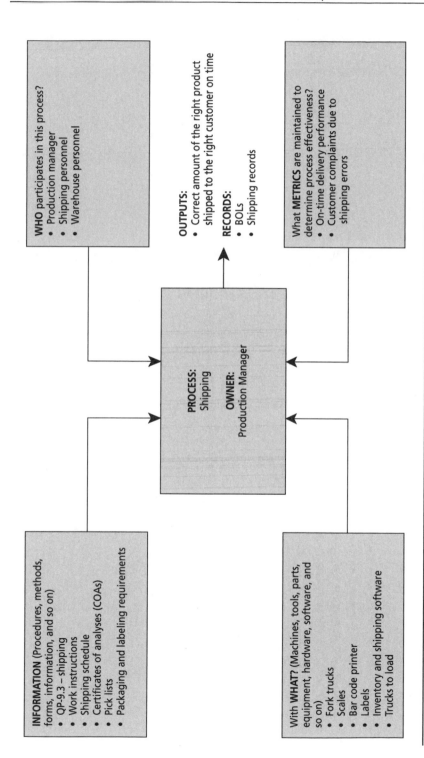

WHO participates in this process?
- Production manager
- Shipping personnel
- Warehouse personnel

OUTPUTS:
- Correct amount of the right product shipped to the right customer on time

RECORDS:
- BOLs
- Shipping records

What **METRICS** are maintained to determine process effectiveness?
- On-time delivery performance
- Customer complaints due to shipping errors

PROCESS:
Shipping

OWNER:
Production Manager

INFORMATION (Procedures, methods, forms, information, and so on)
- QP-9.3 – shipping
- Work instructions
- Shipping schedule
- Certificates of analyses (COAs)
- Pick lists
- Packaging and labeling requirements

With **WHAT?** (Machines, tools, parts, equipment, hardware, software, and so on)
- Fork trucks
- Scales
- Bar code printer
- Labels
- Inventory and shipping software
- Trucks to load

Appendix A Shipping process model.

Appendix B
Checklists for Common Processes

Checklists

- All Processes – These questions are based on the four categories of inputs into every process. Customize this checklist based on the process being audited and then add process-specific questions from the checklists below.

- Calibration

- Continual Improvement Processes (includes customer satisfaction, internal audits, analysis of nonconformances, corrective action, preventive action, and management review)

- Design and Development Control

- Inspection and Testing and Control of Nonconforming Product Processes

- Maintenance

- Management Responsibilities

- Planning for New Products or Processes; Definition of Customer Requirements

- Product or Service Provision; Control of Nonconforming Product

- Purchasing

- Receiving Inspection

QUESTION	EVIDENCE	FOLLOW-UP REQUIRED?	CAR#, IF APPLICABLE
Process Metrics – Clauses 4.1.e/f and 8.2.3 (Reference the METRICS box on the process model)			
1. (Interview the process owner. Ask the following questions:)			
a. What metrics do you keep to evaluate the effectiveness of this process?			
b. Who looks at these metrics? How are they evaluated? Do you have any goals or objectives established?			
c. Are goals and objectives being met? (Pull records to verify whether or not any goals are being achieved.)			
d. (If goals are not being met, ask:) What actions are being taken to improve the process? (Review records to verify that actions are being taken. These actions may be documented on CARs, PARs, in meeting minutes, and so on.)			
e. (If goals are being met, ask:) How are they reviewed for opportunities of continual improvement?			
2. (If applicable, interview any internal customers of the process to determine if the process is effective.)			
Responsibilities, Authorities, Competence, Awareness, and Training – Clause 5.5.1; 6.2 (Reference the WHO box on the process model)			
1. Who participates in this process? (Record those positions to the right that you interviewed in this audit.)			

(Continued)

Appendix B   All processes checklist.

QUESTION	EVIDENCE	FOLLOW-UP REQUIRED?	CAR# IF APPLICABLE
2. How are responsibilities and authorities defined and communicated for these personnel? (These may be in job descriptions, documented procedures or work instructions, and so on. Verify throughout the audit that defined responsibilities and authorities are clearly understood. Note any exceptions to the right.)			
3. Has the organization defined the skills and knowledge (competence) required to perform the jobs in this process?			
4. Where applicable, is training then provided to ensure that employees are competent? What does this process look like?			
5. (Pull training records for employees, either new to the organization or new to the position. Be sure to pull records for management, technical, and administrative personnel, as applicable for the process, as well as operators, maintenance, and QA personnel. Complete the training matrix at the end of this checklist.)			
6. How is training evaluated for effectiveness? (Pull records and verify conformance.) Is there anything that should be done to make the training process more effective? (Note any opportunities for improvement to the right.)			
7. (Interview the new employees. Ask the following questions:)			
a. How would you rate the training process on a scale of 1 to 10? (If 7 or below, ask more questions.) What specific knowledge did you need that was not provided? (Verify that specific training was, in fact, not provided. Note the opportunity for improvement to the right.)			

Appendix B   All processes checklist.

(Continued)

QUESTION	EVIDENCE	FOLLOW-UP REQUIRED?	CAR# IF APPLICABLE
b. What training did you wish you had received? Did lack of that training create a problem for you? (Record any opportunities for improvement to the right.)			
Information required for the process – Clauses 4.1.d, 4.2.1 and 4.2.3 (Reference the INFORMATION box on the process model)			
1. What types of documents are used in this process? (Record these on the attached document control matrix. These may include procedures, work instructions, test methods, job descriptions, specifications, prints, check sheets, batch sheets, control plans, and so on.)			
2. (Interview auditees to verify that the documents include the right amount of information. Sample questions might include the following:) a. Were you trained by your procedures and instructions? b. If so, were they helpful to you? c. If not, why not? Are they too long? Too short? Obsolete? Wrong? (Record any opportunities for improvement to the right.)			
3. (Complete the document control matrix to verify control of necessary documentation.)			
4. (During the audit, were any obsolete or invalid documents noted in areas where the document is used? Look particularly at bulletin boards, postings on the wall or near equipment, and so on.)			

Appendix B   All processes checklist.

(Continued)

QUESTION	EVIDENCE	FOLLOW-UP REQUIRED?	CAR#, IF APPLICABLE
5. (Verify that documents of external origin are identified and that their distribution is controlled. List to the right those documents that were verified. External documents may include legal and regulatory requirements, OEM equipment manuals, customer specifications, international and industry-specific standards, and so on.)			
6. What other information is required for this process? (Depending on the process being audited, this may include work orders, inventory levels, purchase requisitions, production schedules, sample schedules, audit schedules, and so on.)			
7. Does information include everything that you need? Is it correct? Do you get it when you need it?			
Equipment, tools, parts, materials, hardware software required for the process – Clauses 6.3 and 6.4 (Reference the WHAT box on the process model)			
1. What equipment, tools, parts, materials, hardware, or software are required for this process?			
2. Is equipment adequately maintained? Are there any repetitive equipment problems?			
3. Are tools adequate for the process?			
4. Are there any repetitive problems associated with any materials used in the process?			
5. Are materials available when needed?			
6. Is any software used in the process adequate to meet the needs of the users?			

Appendix B   All processes checklist.

(Continued)

QUESTION	EVIDENCE	FOLLOW-UP REQUIRED?	CAR#, IF APPLICABLE
7. Is the work environment suitable for the process?			
Control of Records – Clause 4.2.4 (Reference the OUTPUTS of the process on the process model)			
1. (Throughout the audit, verify that records being presented to the auditor have been identified as records in procedures or other documentation. Note any exceptions to the right.)			
2. (Throughout the audit, verify that records are legible, readily retrievable, and stored in a way that protects their fitness for use. Have responsibilities for record collection and maintenance been clearly defined and documented? Are they understood?)			
3. Where records are stored electronically, are they backed up regularly to prevent their loss?			
4. (Verify that records maintained in long-term storage are stored and filed in a disciplined manner.)			
Policy Statement and Supporting Objectives; Communication – Clauses 5.3, 5.4.1, 5.5.3, and 6.2.2.d			
1. (Interview personnel throughout the audit. Ask the following questions:)			
a. Are you aware of the quality policy? Can you state the key concepts in your own words? How does the quality policy relate to your job?			
b. What goals or objectives have been established for this process? Are we achieving our goals? How does what you do impact whether or not we will meet these goals? (Verify that goals and objectives have been communicated to personnel in this process.)			

(Continued)

Appendix B   All processes checklist.

Document control audit matrix

Process audited: _____

Type of document audited	Number of documents observed	Number that were readily available	Number that were properly approved		Number that were the current issue	Number with the nature of the latest revision identified	Comments

(Continued)

Appendix B All processes checklist.

New employee training audit matrix

New employee	Were competence requirements defined (for example: skills and knowledge needed for the job)?	Was required training provided?	Was effectiveness of training evaluated?	Did training include knowledge of company objectives and the employee's impact on them?	Comments

Appendix B   All processes checklist.

QUESTION	EVIDENCE	FOLLOW-UP REQUIRED?	CAR# IF APPLICABLE
Control of Measuring and Monitoring Devices – Clause 7.6 (This checklist is to be used in conjunction with the "All Processes" checklist)			
1. Describe the calibration process at your organization. Does it include both process and product testing equipment? Does the calibration process include any quality-critical equipment owned by others?			
2. Are standards used to calibrate instruments traceable to a nationally recognized standard? If not, is the basis used for calibration clearly documented? (Pull Certificates of Traceability – or other basis for calibration – for five standards used in the calibration process.)			
3. (In each area responsible for calibration, select up to five instruments and verify the requirements on the attached calibration audit matrix.)			
4. (Throughout the audit, look for instruments that were found to be out of calibration when they were initially checked. Verify that an assessment of previous results took place and that appropriate action was taken with both the instrument and any products that may have been tested with that instrument.)			
5. (Were any instruments repetitively found to be out of calibration? If so, has corrective action been initiated to resolve the problem?)			
6. Is any applicable software included in the calibration process?			
7. (Throughout the audit, verify that instruments and standards are handled in a way that protects their fitness for use. Verify that they are protected against adjustments that would invalidate calibration settings. Note any exceptions to the right.)			

Appendix B   Calibration checklist

(Continued)

Calibration audit matrix

Area audited: _____

Instrument audited (include unique identification)	Calibration status current?	Any damage or deterioration noted?	Frequency of checks?	Results within acceptable limits?	Is standard used to check this instrument traceable to a nationally recognized standard?	Comments

Appendix B   Calibration checklist.

QUESTION	EVIDENCE	FOLLOW-UP REQUIRED?	CAR# IF APPLICABLE
General Requirements – Measurement, Analysis and Improvement – Clause 8.1 and 8.5.1			
1. Describe the processes at your organization to continually improve the effectiveness of the quality management system. What evidence of improvement can you show me?			
2. What statistical tools are used at your organization to analyze data? (Verify that these tools are being used appropriately.)			
Customer Satisfaction – Clause 8.2.1			
1. How does your organization measure and monitor your customers' perception of your ability to meet their requirements? May I see it please? (Verify that data is being collected in accordance with the plans.)			
2. Who evaluates this data and determines whether or not action is required? (Verify that responsibility to initiate corrective or preventive action is clearly defined and understood.)			
3. What action has been taken based on this information? (Review records showing evidence that any appropriate action is being taken. These records may be in the form of CARs, PARs, management review meeting minutes, quality improvement team meeting minutes, and so on.)			
Internal Audits – Clauses 8.2.2 and 8.5.2			
1. Describe the internal audit process at your organization. How are internal audits planned and conducted? How are they reported? How are any required corrections and corrective actions recorded and tracked?			

Appendix B Continual improvement processes checklist (includes customer satisfaction, internal audits, analysis of nonconformances, corrective action, preventive action, and management review).

(Continued)

QUESTION	EVIDENCE	FOLLOW-UP REQUIRED?	CAR# IF APPLICABLE
2. May I see the internal audit schedule for the previous year? (Verify that audits were scheduled based on the status and importance of the process and based on previous audit results.)			
3. (Pull X audit reports at random from the previous year and verify that they were conducted in accordance with the schedule. Use these audit reports to complete the rest of the internal audit checklist.)			
4. How are auditors qualified? (Pull training records for the auditors who performed the above audits and verify that that they were qualified per the procedure.)			
5. (Verify that auditors who performed to above audits did not audit their own work.)			
6. (Verify that auditor notes provide evidence of conformance as well as nonconformance.)			
7. How are audit results brought to the attention of management personnel responsible for the process audited? (Look for evidence: notes copied on the audit report, minutes of the closing meeting, and so on.)			
8. How are internal audit findings addressed to ensure timely and thorough corrective action to remove nonconformities and their causes? (Pull X findings at random from the previous year and complete the corrective action matrix at the end of this checklist.)			
9. During the previous year, what specific improvements to the business have resulted from the internal audit process? Is there anything that should be done to improve the effectiveness of internal audits?			

Appendix B   Continual improvement processes checklist (includes customer satisfaction, internal audits, analysis of nonconformances, corrective action, preventive action, and management review).

(Continued)

QUESTION	EVIDENCE	FOLLOW-UP REQUIRED?	CAR# IF APPLICABLE
Analysis of Nonconformances – Clauses 8.3, 8.4, and 8.5.2.a			
1. How are product or service nonconformances tracked and monitored for opportunities to reduce them? (Pull corrective actions where indicated and verify that actions are being taken to reduce nonconformances.)			
Corrective Action – Clause 8.5.2			
1. How does the corrective action process work? (Who can initiate a CAR? Who evaluates them? Who tracks them to ensure that they are completed? Who is responsible for making sure that corrective actions are verified as having been effective?)			
2. (Where this has not been done earlier in the checklist, select X Corrective Action Requests from customer complaints, X from internal audit findings, and X from nonconforming product and complete the corrective action matrix at the end of this checklist.)			
Preventive Action – Clause 8..5.3			
1. How is preventive action identified and documented at your organization? (Verify that there is a process to identify proactive, preventive actions.)			
2. (Pull three records of preventive actions and verify conformance to documented procedures.)			
3. In the past year, what specific improvements to the business have resulted from the corrective and preventive action processes (that is: reduced scrap, less rework, fewer customer complaints, more efficient processes, more streamlined processes, higher customer satisfaction results, and so on)?			

Appendix B Continual improvement processes checklist (includes customer satisfaction, internal audits, analysis of nonconformances, corrective action, preventive action, and management review).

(Continued)

QUESTION	EVIDENCE	FOLLOW-UP REQUIRED?	CAR#, IF APPLICABLE
Management Review – Clause 5.6; 6.1			
1. Describe the management review process. Who are the required attendees? How often does the review take place? What data is assessed? How is the meeting recorded? (Select X management review records and verify the following:)			
2. Were they conducted at the required frequency?			
3. Were the required attendees present?			
4. Were the required agenda items and objectives discussed at each review? (Verify that the following specific items were reviewed:) a. Results of audits – both internal and external b. Customer feedback (may include customer complaints and concerns as well as customer satisfaction data) c. Metrics related to process performance; metrics related to conformance with product or service specifications d. Status of corrective and preventive actions e. Follow-up actions from previous management reviews f. Planned changes that could affect the quality management system (for example, planned re-organizations, new processes, new products, major changes in the marketplace, and so on) g. Recommendations for improvement h. Review of the policy and objectives to assess opportunities for improvement and the need for any changes			

Appendix B Continual improvement processes checklist (includes customer satisfaction, internal audits, analysis of nonconformances, corrective action, preventive action, and management review). *(Continued)*

QUESTION	EVIDENCE	FOLLOW-UP REQUIRED?	CAR#, IF APPLICABLE
5. Do records include resulting decisions and actions? (Select X action items at random from the reviews and verify that they were completed and that action taken was effective.)			
6. During the past year, what specific improvements to the quality system, its processes, and product/service have been initiated or made as a result of management review? Have resource requirements been adequately addressed?			

Appendix B Continual improvement processes checklist (includes customer satisfaction, internal audits, analysis of nonconformances, corrective action, preventive action, and management review).

(Continued)

Corrective action audit matrix

Corrective action request number	Was the cause of the problem identified?	Was action taken to eliminate the cause?	Is there evidence that action taken was effective?	Were any associated documents updated as a result of action?	Was corrective action completed without undue delay?	Comments

Appendix B Continual improvement processes checklist (includes customer satisfaction, internal audits, analysis of nonconformances, corrective action, preventive action, and management review).

QUESTION	EVIDENCE	FOLLOW-UP REQUIRED?	CAR#, IF APPLICABLE
Design and Development Control – Clause 7.3 (This checklist is to be used in conjunction with the "All Processes" checklist)			
1. Describe the design and development process.			
2. (Select X recently closed projects and verify the following:)			
a. Was there a design plan for each project?			
b. Did plans identify specific activities and the individual responsible for completing them?			
c. Did plans include the review, verification, and validation activities that are appropriate to each stage of the design?			
d. Who were the interfaces that were identified for each project? How were they kept abreast of the status of the design? (Pull records to verify conformance.)			
e. Was the plan updated as necessary as the project evolved?			
f. Were customer and regulatory requirements clearly defined for each project along with the functional and performance requirements for the product? Were these requirements reviewed and approved? (Pull evidence.)			
g. Were "lessons learned" from previous projects reviewed at the beginning of each project?			
h. Is there evidence for each project that the design output (that is, prints, drawings, specifications, verification and validation results, and so on) met the customer and regulatory requirements specified in the question above?			
i. Did design output include or reference acceptance criteria?			
j. Do the output documents specify the characteristics of the product that are essential for its safe and proper use?			

Appendix B *Design and development control checklist.*

(Continued)

QUESTION	EVIDENCE	FOLLOW-UP REQUIRED?	CAR#, IF APPLICABLE
k. Are records available to show evidence of design review for each project at the required intervals? Were appropriate functions involved in each review? Were follow-up activities recorded?			
l. Were verification requirements clearly defined and documented? (Pull records and verify that requirements were successfully completed or that follow-up activities were recorded.)			
m. Were validation requirements clearly defined and documented? (Pull validation records and verify that requirements were successfully completed or follow-up activities were recorded.)			
n. Have any of the projects had changes? (If so, verify that they were reviewed, verified, validated, and approved as appropriate.) Was the effect of the change on other parts or the finished product evaluated? Do records include the results of the review as well as any necessary actions?			
3. (Interview the "customers" of the design and development process to ensure that the output is providing adequate information to operations, purchasing, maintenance, QA, and so on. Ask:)			
a. Are operations personnel receiving adequate information to run the process?			
b. Are purchasing personnel receiving adequate information (on raw material specs, and so on) in time to order acceptable materials from qualified suppliers?			
c. Are QA personnel receiving adequate information in time to effectively test the new product?			
d. Are maintenance personnel receiving adequate information to effectively maintain the equipment?			

Appendix B   Design and development control checklist.

QUESTION	EVIDENCE	FOLLOW-UP REQUIRED?	CAR#, IF APPLICABLE
Monitoring and Measurement of Product – Clause 8.2.4 (This checklist is to be used in conjunction with the "All Processes" checklist)			
1. What in-process product inspection or testing is performed at your organization?			
2. (Select X in-process parts and/or materials at random and verify that defined requirements were met.)			
3. Did in-process parts and/or materials meet specified requirements? If not, were they controlled and dispositioned in accordance with the Control of Nonconforming Product procedure?			
4. Is the individual who released acceptable parts or materials identified in the records?			
5. What final product inspection and testing is performed at your organization?			
6. (Select X final products at random and verify that defined requirements were met.)			
7. Did final products meet specified requirements? If not, were they identified, controlled and dispositioned in accordance with the Control of Nonconforming Product procedure?			
8. Is the individual who released acceptable parts or materials identified in the records?			

Appendix B Inspection and testing and control of nonconforming product processes checklist.　　　　　*(Continued)*

QUESTION	EVIDENCE	FOLLOW-UP REQUIRED?	CAR#, IF APPLICABLE
Control of Nonconforming Product			
1. How are nonconforming incoming materials, in-process materials, and final products controlled to prevent them from being shipped or further processed without required approval?			
2. (Walk through production and storage areas and verify conformance with documented procedures. Record any exceptions to the right.)			
3. Who has the authority to approve or disposition nonconforming parts and materials? (Pull records for X nonconforming parts or materials and verify that the disposition was made and documented by the authorized personnel.)			
4. (Where nonconforming part or materials are noted, do records provide evidence of the nature of the nonconformity and any subsequent actions taken?)			
5. (Visit production and storage areas to verify that any nonconforming product is suitably identified and controlled per the procedure.)			
6. (If nonconforming product was detected after shipment, was appropriate action taken?)			

Appendix B   Inspection and testing and control of nonconforming product processes checklist.

QUESTION	EVIDENCE	FOLLOW-UP REQUIRED?	CAR#, IF APPLICABLE
Maintenance – Clause 6.3 (This checklist is to be used in conjunction with the "All Processes" checklist)			
1. Describe the maintenance process. Does it include preventive, predictive, and emergency maintenance as appropriate?			
2. How is preventive maintenance (PM) scheduled? May I see the PM schedule please? (Pull X equipment records and verify conformance to the PM schedule.)			
3. How is Maintenance notified of equipment failure and the need for emergency maintenance? (If work orders are used, ask:) Do maintenance personnel receive adequate information on the work order to repair the equipment in a timely manner?			

Appendix B   Maintenance checklist.

QUESTION	EVIDENCE	FOLLOW-UP REQUIRED?	CAR#, IF APPLICABLE
Management Responsibilities – Clauses 5.1 – 5.4 (Management review is addressed in the "Continual Improvement" checklist)			
1. (Interview senior management at your organization to verify commitment to the quality management system. Use the questions below as a guide.)			
a. What is the policy statement for your organization? (Verify that it was approved by senior management.)			
b. Does it specify a commitment to continual improvement of the quality management process? How can that commitment be demonstrated?			
c. How does it provide a framework for supporting objectives?			
d. How is it reviewed for continued suitability? (Pull records to verify conformance.)			
e. How have you communicated the policy throughout the organization?			
f. What measurable goals or objectives have been established to support the policy and verify the effective performance of the quality management system?			
g. How is the importance of conforming to customer requirements communicated throughout the facility?			
h. How are objectives "pushed down" throughout the organization? (Verify conformance.)			
i. How are objectives tracked and monitored?			
j. Are objectives being achieved? (Pull records showing whether or not objectives are being achieved.)			

(Continued)

Appendix B   Management checklist.

QUESTION	EVIDENCE	FOLLOW-UP REQUIRED?	CAR# IF APPLICABLE
k. (If objectives are not being achieved, ask:) What actions are being taken? (Pull records of actions taken. These may be in the form of Corrective Action Requests, Preventive Action Requests, meeting minutes, and so on.)			
l. (If objectives are being achieved, ask:) How are they reviewed for opportunities of continual improvement?			
Management Representative – Clause 5.5.2			
1. (Is there a clearly defined Management Representative? Is he/she a member of management?)			
2. (How does the Management Representative ensure the promotion of awareness of customer requirements throughout the facility?)			
3. (Are the Management Representative's roles and responsibilities clearly defined in the documented system? Do they include implementation and maintenance of the quality management system, as well as communicating information to top management about the effectiveness of the quality management system?)			

Appendix B   Management checklist.

QUESTION	EVIDENCE	FOLLOW-UP REQUIRED?	CAR# IF APPLICABLE
Planning for New Products and Processes – Clause 7.1 (This checklist is to be used in conjunction with the "All Processes" checklist)			
1. Describe how your organization defines and documents customer requirements.			
2. (Select X recent new or changed products or processes and verify the following:)			
a. How were product or service requirements and quality objectives defined? May I see them please?			
b. How were current processes, documentation, and resources evaluated to ensure that they were suitable for the new product or process? (Look for evidence that any identified action items were completed.)			
c. How were verification, validation, inspection, and test requirements defined? Did they include acceptance criteria? May I see what was defined for these?			
d. Were any new records identified that would be necessary for these products, processes, or projects?			
Definition and review of customer requirements – Clause 7.2			
1. Does documentation (for example, customer contracts, RFQs, RFPs, product specifications, packaging standards, orders, and so on) clearly and adequately define customer requirements including delivery and post-delivery requirements?			
2. Do defined requirements include product-related statutory and regulatory requirements and any other requirement not necessarily stated by the customer but required for the product's known and intended use? May I see examples?			

(Continued)

Appendix B   Planning for new products or processes; definition of customer requirements checklist.

QUESTION	EVIDENCE	FOLLOW-UP REQUIRED?	CAR#, IF APPLICABLE
3. (Pull X examples of new products/customers at random to verify conformance to questions 1 and 2. Note the orders reviewed to the right.)			
4. Who is responsible for reviewing customer requirements prior to accepting the order to verify that your organization has the capability of meeting those requirements? (Verify that the documents above contain evidence of review and acceptance.)			
5. If your organization cannot meet the customer's requirements – including ship date – or if requirements on the order are difference from those on the contract, how is that resolved with the customer? By whom? What records are kept? (Pull records to verify conformance.)			
6. How are changes to customer requirements reviewed? By whom? What records are maintained? How are affected employees notified of the changes? (Pull records to verify conformance.)			
7. (Review the customer complaint file to look for possible repetitive complaints that are the result of unclear customer requirements or requirements that your organization could not meet. Be sure to include delivery and service performance as well as product nonconformances. Note any opportunities for improvement to the right.)			

Appendix B   Planning for new products or processes; definition of customer requirements checklist.

QUESTION	EVIDENCE	FOLLOW-UP REQUIRED?	CAR#, IF APPLICABLE
Product or Service Provision (This checklist is to be used in conjunction with the "All Processes" checklist)			
1. How is production scheduled to ensure that ship dates or delivery dates are met? Is the schedule appropriate? Is it realistic or does does meeting it often require extraordinary measures?			
2. What measurement or monitoring activities are required in the process? May I see them please? (Select X measurements and verify the following questions:)			
a. Are acceptance limits defined and documented? Are they available to the operator?			
b. (Pull records at random from the past several months. Do records show evidence that the parameters are within specified limits? If not, was action taken as specified in the procedures? Record records reviewed and results found to the right.)			
3. Describe the process for releasing and shipping product to ensure that only acceptable product is shipped to the correct customer. (Verify conformance to procedures.)			
Verification of Processes for Production and Service Provision – Clause 7.5.2			
1. Does your organization have any processes in which the final product cannot be verified by subsequent monitoring and measurement? (If not, delete this section of the checklist.) How are these processes validated to demonstrate that planned results are achieved?			

Appendix B   Product or service provision; control of nonconforming product checklist.

(Continued)

QUESTION	EVIDENCE	FOLLOW-UP REQUIRED?	CAR#, IF APPLICABLE
2. (Verify that this validation includes the following:)			
a. Defined criteria for review and approval of the process. (Pull records to verify conformance.)			
b. Approval of equipment and qualification of personnel. (Pull records to verify conformance.)			
c. Use of specific methods and procedures.			
d. Requirements for records.			
e. Revalidation requirements. (Pull records to verify conformance.)			
Identification and Traceability – Clause 7.5.3			
1. How are incoming materials, in-process materials, and final products clearly identified?			
2. (Walk through storage and production areas to verify conformance to the procedures. Note any exceptions to the right.)			
3. What are the traceability requirements for your organization? (Pull records to verify conformance to traceability requirements.)			
4. How is inspection and test status of incoming materials, in-process materials, and final products identified?			
5. (Walk through the facility and verify conformance to procedures.)			

Appendix B Product or service provision; control of nonconforming product checklist.

(Continued)

QUESTION	EVIDENCE	FOLLOW-UP REQUIRED?	CAR# IF APPLICABLE
Customer Property – Clause 7.5.4			
1. What customer-supplied products does your organization receive, if any? How are these products inspected upon receipt to ensure that they are fit for use? (Note that customer-supplied product can include raw materials, in-process parts, dies, shipping containers, intellectual property, and so on.)			
2. (Pull receiving records to verify conformance to receiving inspection requirements.)			
3. How are customer-supplied products protected and safeguarded to protect their fitness for use? (Walk through storage areas to look for evidence of conformance to procedures.)			
4. What process is in place to notify customers of any problems associated with their property?			
Preservation of Product – Clause 7.5.5			
1. How are products handled and stored to protect their fitness for use? (For example, what specific handling and storage issues do you have at your organization? Electrostatic discharge concerns? Shelf lives on products, materials, or lab reagents? Fork truck damage? Temperature and/or humidity of storage areas? Double and triple stacking of cartons that crush the bottom carton? Torn bags in storage?)			
2. (Pull records as required and walk through storage areas to verify conformance to procedures.)			

Appendix B Product or service provision; control of nonconforming product checklist.

(Continued)

QUESTION	EVIDENCE	FOLLOW-UP REQUIRED?	CAR#, IF APPLICABLE
Control of Nonconforming Product – Clause 8.3			
1. How are nonconforming incoming materials, in-process materials, and final products controlled to prevent them from being shipped or further processed without defined approval?			
2. (Walk through production and storage areas to verify conformance to the documented procedure. Specifically look for any labeling or segregation requirements.)			
Work Environment – Clause 6.4			
1. (Verify throughout the audit that the appropriate work environment exists to achieve conformity to customer requirements. Examples may include appropriate lighting in production and inspection areas, housekeeping issues, inappropriate heat or humidity, and so on.)			

Appendix B   Product or service provision; control of nonconforming product checklist.

QUESTION	EVIDENCE	FOLLOW-UP REQUIRED?	CAR#, IF APPLICABLE
Purchasing – Clause 7.4 (This checklist is to be used in conjunction with the "All Processes" checklist)			
1. Describe the purchasing process. How are suppliers of quality-related goods and services evaluated and approved?			
2. Are qualification requirements for new suppliers clearly defined and documented? May I see them please? (Pull X current supplier records and verify that they provide evidence of conformance to requirements. If any suppliers have been approved in the past year, review their records to verify that they met qualification requirements.)			
3. How are suppliers re-evaluated? (Review records to verify conformance to specified requirements. Where records show evidence of poor performance, follow through to ensure that corrective action has been initiated.)			
4. How does your organization identify qualified suppliers (Approved Supplier List, Purchasing software, and so on)? May I see it? (Use this list in evaluating the purchasing documents below.)			
5. (Review X Purchase Orders or your organization's purchasing documents and verify the following:)			
a. Were they issued to suppliers that have met the selection and evaluation criteria?			
b. Were the products or services being ordered clearly defined along with required delivery dates, any required quality system standards, applicable approval requirements, and personnel qualification, as applicable?			
c. Were the Purchase Orders reviewed to ensure their adequacy prior to being issued?			

Appendix B   Purchasing checklist.

QUESTION	EVIDENCE	FOLLOW-UP REQUIRED?	CAR#, IF APPLICABLE
Receiving Inspection – Clause 7.4.3 (This checklist is to be used in conjunction with the "All Processes" checklist)			
1. Describe the receiving inspection process.			
2. (Select X incoming materials at random and verify that inspection requirements were met.)			
3. Did all incoming materials meet specified requirements? If not, how are they controlled to ensure that they were not used until receiving proper authorization?			
4. (Review records of nonconformances in production. Are there a large number that are due to incoming materials? If yes, follow through to determine whether there are opportunities to improve the receiving inspection process.)			

Appendix B Receiving inspection checklist.

Appendix C

Audit Preparation Example

Contents

- Acme Equipment Maintenance Procedure
- Acme Maintenance Audit Checklist

QUALITY PROCEDURE
EQUIPMENT MAINTENANCE

Purpose

The purpose of this procedure is to describe the process for ensuring that manufacturing equipment is properly maintained. The desired output of this process is to minimize unscheduled downtime of manufacturing equipment.

Application

This procedure applies to the all process equipment at the Acme manufacturing facility.

Procedure

1. Operators at Acme are responsible for performing daily and weekly preventive maintenance on the process equipment (such as lubrication and so on). These activities are described in the Operators' Work Instructions. Records are maintained on equipment log sheets located at each piece of equipment.

2. Maintenance technicians are responsible for performing monthly, semi-annual, and annual preventive maintenance activities. These PM requirements are defined on the PM schedule and are recorded in the equipment files in Maintenance. Equipment files are maintained in the GaugeTrak software system.

3. Where outside contractors are responsible for routine PM activities, these activities are also defined on the PM schedule. The Maintenance Manager is responsible for scheduling these activities with the appropriate subcontractor and ensuring conformance to the PM Schedule. Records are maintained in the equipment files in Maintenance. Qualified subcontractors are defined on the Approved Suppliers List in Purchasing and are communicated to the Maintenance Manager via the SAP system.

4. When equipment failures occur, the Operations Supervisor is responsible for completing the Maintenance Work Order and forwarding it to the Maintenance Planner. The Maintenance Planner schedules/prioritizes maintenance activities based on the information provided on the Work Order.

5. Spare parts for key manufacturing equipment are maintained in the stock room. The stock room maintains an inventory of parts in accordance with the stock room work instructions for inventory control. The inventory of parts is based on a "min/max" system in SAP. For each critical part, a minimum and maximum inventory level is identified within SAP. As parts are removed from the stock room, Maintenance personnel are responsible for bar coding those parts to adjust the inventory levels in the SAP system. When the minimum inventory level is reached, SAP will generate a PO and forward to Purchasing personnel to re-stock the part.

Records

Equipment log sheets in Production, equipment files in Maintenance, completed work orders, maintenance subcontractor qualifications, and inventory of spare part records are maintained in accordance with QP-16-01, Control of Records.

Associated Documents

QP-06-01, Purchasing
QP-16-01, Control of Records
OEM Equipment Manuals
Operators' Work Instructions
PM Log Sheet Form

QUESTION	EVIDENCE	FOLLOW-UP REQUIRED?	CAR#, IF APPLICABLE
Process Metrics – Clause 8.2.3 and 4.1.e/f (Reference the METRICS box on the process model)			
1. Interview the Maintenance Manager. Ask the following questions: a. What metrics do you keep to evaluate the effectiveness of Maintenance? b. Who looks at these metrics? How are they evaluated? Do you have any goals or objectives established? c. Are goals and objectives being met? (Pull records to verify whether or not any goals are being achieved.) d. (If goals are not being met, ask:) What actions are being taken to improve the process? (Review records to verify that actions are being taken. These actions may be documented on CARs, PARs, in meeting minutes, and so on.) e. (If goals are being met, ask:) How are they reviewed for opportunities of continual improvement?			
2. (Interview manufacturing personnel to determine whether the maintenance process is effective. Record any opportunities for improvement to the right.)			
Responsibilities, Authorities, Competence, Awareness, and Training – Clause 5.5.1; 6.2 (Reference the WHO box on the process model)			
1. Who performs required maintenance on the equipment?			
2. How are responsibilities and authorities defined and communicated for these personnel? (Verify throughout the audit that defined responsibilities and authorities are clearly understood. Be sure to include any responsibilities for operations personnel as well as Maintenance personnel. Note any exceptions to the right.)			

(Continued)

Appendix C Acme maintenance audit checklist.

QUESTION	EVIDENCE	FOLLOW-UP REQUIRED?	CAR# IF APPLICABLE
3. Has Acme defined the skills and knowledge (competence) required to perform the jobs in Maintenance? Is training provided to ensure that employees are competent?			
4. (Pull training records for new employees – either new to Acme or new to the position. Be sure to pull records for appropriate operations and engineering personnel in addition to Maintenance personnel. Verify the following:)			
a. Were competence requirements and training needs defined for each position in the WHO box of the process model?			
b. Was training provided to meet those needs? (If not, how was competence verified? Pull records to verify conformance to required training needs.)			
c. Did the training include awareness of the importance of the employee's activities in achieving Acme's quality policy and objectives?			
d. How were these individuals deemed competent to perform the job?			
5. How is the training of Maintenance personnel evaluated for effectiveness? (Pull records and verify conformance.) Should something be done to make the training process more effective? (Note any opportunities for improvement to the right.)			
6. (Interview the new employees. These may include employees new to Acme or just new to Maintenance. Ask the following questions:)			
a. How would you rate the training process on a scale of 1 to 10? (If 7 or below, ask:) What specific knowledge did you need that you did not get? (If applicable, verify that training needs do not include the training omission. If not, note the opportunity for improvement to the right.)			

Appendix C   Acme maintenance audit checklist.

(Continued)

QUESTION	EVIDENCE	FOLLOW-UP REQUIRED?	CAR#, IF APPLICABLE
Process Metrics – Clause 8.2.3 and 4.1.e/f (Reference the METRICS box on the process model)			
1. (Interview the Maintenance Manager. Ask the following questions:)			
a. What metrics do you keep to evaluate the effectiveness of Maintenance?			
b. Who looks at these metrics? How are they evaluated? Do you have any goals or objectives established?			
c. Are goals and objectives being met? (Pull records to verify whether or not any goals are being achieved.)			
d. (If goals are not being met, ask:) What actions are being taken to improve the process? (Review records to verify that actions are being taken. These actions may be documented on CARs, PARs, in meeting minutes, and so on.)			
e. (If goals are being met, ask:) How are they reviewed for opportunities of continual improvement?			
2. (Interview manufacturing personnel to determine whether the maintenance process is effective. Record any opportunities for improvement to the right.)			
Responsibilities, Authorities, Competence, Awareness, and Training – Clause 5.5.1; 6.2 (Reference the WHO box on the process model)			
1. Who performs required maintenance on the equipment?			
2. How are responsibilities and authorities defined and communicated for these personnel? (Verify throughout the audit that defined responsibilities and authorities are clearly understood. Be sure to include any responsibilities for operations personnel as well as Maintenance personnel. Note any exceptions to the right.)			

(Continued)

Appendix C   Acme maintenance audit checklist.

QUESTION	EVIDENCE	FOLLOW-UP REQUIRED?	CAR#, IF APPLICABLE
3. Has Acme defined the skills and knowledge (competence) required to perform the jobs in Maintenance? Is training provided to ensure that employees are competent?			
4. (Pull training records for new employees – either new to Acme or new to the position. Be sure to pull records for appropriate operations and engineering personnel in addition to Maintenance personnel. Verify the following:) a. Were competence requirements and training needs defined for each position in the WHO box of the process model? b. Was training provided to meet those needs? (If not, how was competence verified? Pull records to verify conformance to required training needs.) c. Did the training include awareness of the importance of the employee's activities in achieving Acme's quality policy and objectives? d. How were these individuals deemed competent to perform the job?			
5. How is the training of Maintenance personnel evaluated for effectiveness? (Pull records and verify conformance.) Should something be done to make the training process more effective? (Note any opportunities for improvement to the right.)			
6. (Interview the new employees. These may include employees new to Acme or just new to Maintenance. Ask the following questions:) a. How would you rate the training process on a scale of 1 to 10? (If 7 or below, ask:) What specific knowledge did you need that you did not get? (If applicable, verify that training needs do not include the training omission. If not, note the opportunity for improvement to the right.)			

(Continued)

Appendix C Acme maintenance audit checklist.

QUESTION	EVIDENCE	FOLLOW-UP REQUIRED?	CAR#, IF APPLICABLE
b. What training do you wish you had received that was not provided? Did that lack of training create a problem for you? (Again, record any opportunities for improvement to the right.)			
Information required for the process – Clause 4.2.1 and 4.2.3 (Reference the INFORMATION box on the process model)			
1. What types of documents are used in Maintenance? (Record these on the attached document control matrix. These may include the preventive maintenance (PM) schedule, Operator Work Instructions, OEM equipment manuals, and so on.)			
2. (Complete the document control matrix to verify control of necessary documentation.)			
3. (Pull equipment log sheets from Production and equipment files in GaugeTrak. Have equipment maintenance requirements specified in the Operators Work Instructions and PM Schedule been met? Record results of this review to the right.)			
4. (During the audit, were any obsolete or invalid documents noted in areas where the document is used? Look particularly at bulletin boards, postings on the wall or near equipment, and so on.)			
5. (Verify that any documents of external origin, such as OEM equipment manuals, are identified and their distribution is controlled. List to the right those documents that were verified.)			
6. What other information is required for this process (such as work orders, Approved Suppliers List for maintenance subcontractors, and so on)?			

Appendix C Acme maintenance audit checklist.

(Continued)

QUESTION	EVIDENCE	FOLLOW-UP REQUIRED?	CAR#, IF APPLICABLE
7. Do maintenance work orders include everything that you need to know? Are they correct? Do you get them when you need them to minimize downtime?			
8. Do you have access to the current Approved Suppliers List for Maintenance subcontractors in SAP? How were these subcontractors evaluated? May I see the records?			
Equipment, tools, parts, materials, hardware software required for the process – Clauses 6.3 and 6.4 (Reference the WHAT box on the process model)			
1. What equipment, tools, parts, materials, hardware, or software are required for the Maintenance process?			
2. Are tools adequate for the process? Are they available when they are needed?			
3. Are spare parts available when they are needed? How often have you been to the stock room to get spare parts for equipment, could not find them, and had to keep manufacturing equipment down until parts could be procured? (If downtime due to unavailable spare parts is excessive, pull records to verify and record as an opportunity for improvement to the right.)			
4. Is GaugeTrak adequate to meet the needs of the users? Is it user-friendly? Is there information that you need that is not currently in the system?			
5. Is the work environment suitable for Maintenance?			

(Continued)

Appendix C   Acme maintenance audit checklist.

QUESTION	EVIDENCE	FOLLOW-UP REQUIRED?	CAR#, IF APPLICABLE
Control of Records – Clause 4.2.4 (Reference the OUTPUTS of the process on the process model)			
1. (Throughout the audit, verify that records being presented to the auditor have been identified as records in procedures or other documentation. Note any exceptions to the right.)			
2. (Throughout the audit, verify that records are legible, readily retrievable, and stored in a way that protects their fitness for use. Have responsibilities for record collection and maintenance been clearly defined and documented? Are they understood?)			
3. Where records are stored electronically, are they backed up regularly to prevent their loss? May I see evidence of that?			
4. (Verify that records maintained in long-term storage are stored and filed in a disciplined manner.)			
Policy Statement and Supporting Objectives; Communication – Clauses 5.3, 5.4.1, 5.5.3, and 6.2.2.d			
1. (Interview personnel throughout the audit. Ask the following questions:)			
a. Are you aware of the quality policy? Can you state the key concepts in your own words? How does it relate to your job?			
b. What goals or objectives have been established for the Maintenance process? Are we achieving our goals? How does what you do impact whether or not we will meet these goals? (Verify that goals and objectives have been communicated to personnel in this process.)			

Appendix C   Acme maintenance audit checklist.

(Continued)

Document control audit matrix

Process audited: _____

Type of document audited	Number of documents observed	Number that were readily available	Number that were properly approved	Number that were the current issue	Number with the nature of the latest revision identified	Comments
Operator work instructions that include equipment maintenance requirements						
PM Schedule			N/A			
OEM Manuals			N/A			

Appendix C Acme maintenance audit checklist.

Appendix D
Internal Audit Forms

Process

- Process Audit Matrix
- Audit Summary Report
- Audit Action Item List
- Corrective Action Log
- Corrective Action Request (CAR)

ISO 9001:2008 Clause	Management	Inspection	Calibration	Production	Purchasing	Shipping	Design Control	Sales	Order Entry	Maintenance	Continual Improvement
Clause 5 – Management Responsibilities	X	X	E	O	E	O	E	O	E	E	X
Clause 6.1 – Resource Man.	X										
Clauses 7.1 & 7.5 – Production Planning and Product / Service Provision		X		X		X	X		X	X	
Clause 7.2 – Customer Processes		O	E	O				X	X		
Clause 7.3 – Design & Development Control			O	E	O			X	X	E	
Clause 7.4 – Purchasing		X	X	X	E					O	
Clause 7.6 – Calibration		X	X							X	
Clauses 8.1, 8.2.1 – General and Customer Satisfaction											X
Clause 8.2.2 – Internal Audit											X
Clause 8.5 – Corrective & Preventive Action	A	A	A	A	A	A	A	A	A	A	X
Clauses 8.2.4 – Inspection & Testing		X		X							X
Clause 8.3 – Control of Nonconforming Product		X		X							

- Clauses 4.1, 4.2.1, 4.2.2, 4.2.3, 4.2.4, 6.2, 6.3, 6.4, 8.2.3, and 8.4 are audited with each process audit.
- X = this department plays a key role in the process(es) being audited and should be audited every year.
- E, O = these departments play a more peripheral role in process(es) being audited and can be audited every other year (E = even-numbered years; O = odd-numbered years).
- A = as applicable

Appendix D   Process audit matrix.

To:

An audit of the _____ process within the quality management system was performed on _____. Departments involved in the audit included:

_____

_____

The auditors included:

_____   _____

A summary of the findings is given below:

CAR: Brief description

_____   _____

_____   _____

_____   _____

_____   _____

_____   _____

Observations are recorded on the attached Audit Action Item List

Opportunities for improvement included:

_____

_____

_____

Examples of continual improvement noted since the last audit included:

_____

_____

_____

_____

Thank you very much for your cooperation in making this audit a success. Please remember that Corrective Action Requests are due back to me with proposed action items and estimated completion dates by_____.

Thank you,

Appendix D   Audit summary report.

Action item	Audit date	Assigned to	Action taken	Date completed	Verification date

Appendix D   Audit action item list.

CAR #	Date initiated	Assigned to	Estimated completion date	Actual completion date	Planned verification date	Actual verification date

Appendix D Corrective action log.

Corrective Action Request (CAR)

CAR #: _____   Reason
                                     ☐ Internal Audit
Date:_____   ☐ External Audit
                                     ☐ Customer Complaint
Initiator: _____   ☐ Product Nonconformity
                                     ☐ Other: _____

Describe the problem:

Probable root cause:

Management Representative Approval:

Action Plan:

Estimated completion date: _____   Actual Completion date: _____

Verification of effectiveness (record of EVIDENCE that corrective action has been effective or reference a new CAR #)

Have associated documents been updated as necessary?   ☐ yes   ☐ no

Signed: _____   Date:_____

Appendix D   Corrective Action Request (CAR).

Appendix E

Revisions Related to ISO 9001:2008

Changes to clauses 4-8 of ISO 9001:2008 are summarized below. Detailed revisions in wording can be found in Annex B of the ISO 9001:2008 standard.

ISO 9001:2008 Reference	Description of the Change
4.1 – General requirements	"Where applicable" has been added to clarify process measures. Author's note: Be careful in implementing this change not to eliminate valuable process metrics. This addition was intended to eliminate the need for a metric in the rare event that a process metric would add no value to the organization.
	Notes 2 and 3 were added to clarify the definition of an outsourced process and provide a list of factors that may help define the "type and extent" of control over these processes.
4.2.1 – General (Documentation requirements)	Minor wording changes only to incorporate "records" into the requirements of "c" and "d." As such, "e" from ISO 9001:2000 was removed as it was no longer needed.
	Note 1 was clarified to state that how an organization chooses to document the required procedures is at the discretion of the organization. A single procedure may be used to document two processes (such as Corrective and Preventive Action) or multiple procedures may be used to document a single process.
4.2.3.f – Control of documents	External documents were clarified to state that they are only those that the organization identifies as necessary to the effective functioning of the quality management system.
5.5.2 – Management representative	A revision was made to clarify that the management representative must be a member of the organization's management.

ISO 9001:2008 Reference	Description of the Change
6.2.1 – General (Human resources)	The text was revised and a note added to clarify that any employee who either directly or indirectly affects the organization's ability to meet product requirements and/or performs tasks required by the quality management system should be included in the training process. Author's note: This could include anyone from sales, design, order entry, project management, purchasing, engineering, management, and so on.
6.2.2 – Competence, training, and awareness	Again, changes were made in "a" and "b" to clarify that training or other activities must take place to achieve the necessary competence of any employee who impacts the organization's ability to conform to product requirements.
6.3 – Infrastructure	"Information systems" was added to those supporting services listed in "c."
6.4 – Work environment	A note was added to clarify conditions that may impact the work environment.
7.2.1 – Determination of requirements related to the product	A note was added to define post-delivery activities.
7.3.1 – Design and development planning	A note was added to clarify that though design and development review, verification, and validation have separate and distinct purposes, they may be conducted and recorded separately or in any combination as it applies to the organization. Author's note: For example, design review, verification, and validation would look quite different in a chemical company when compared to a carton manufacturer where carton design may take from 15 minutes to several hours to complete.
7.3.3 – Design & development outputs	A note has been added to clarify that design and development outputs may include details for preservation of product.
7.5.3 – Identification and traceability	Additions were made to state that monitoring and measurement status should be identified throughout product realization.
	The requirement for records of traceability was also added where traceability is a requirement for the organization.
7.5.4 – Customer property	The note was clarified to add "personal data" as an example of customer property.
7.5.5 – Preservation of product	Preservation of product was clarified to indicate that its purpose is to maintain conformity to requirements (as applicable).

ISO 9001:2008 Reference	Description of the Change
7.6 – Control of monitoring and measuring equipment	Monitoring and measuring of "devices" has been changed to monitoring and measuring of "equipment." The note referring to ISO 10012 was removed. A note was added to clarify how the ability of software to meet intended applications could be confirmed.
8.1.a – General (Measurement, analysis, and improvement)	Wording was changed from "conformity of the product" to "conformity to product requirements."
8.2.1 – Customer satisfaction	A note was added to describe methods by which an organization may monitor customer perception.
8.2.2 – Internal audit	An addition was made to clarify that records of internal audits must be maintained. ISO 9001:2008 adds a provision now for "corrections" following an internal audit in addition to "corrective actions." Reference to ISO 10011 in the note has been updated to ISO 19011.
8.2.3 – Monitoring and measurement of processes	The reference "to ensure conformity of the product" was removed. Author's note: This removes some of the confusion around whether 8.2.3 was referring to only manufacturing processes. With this clarification, it is apparent that 8.2.3 refers to all processes in the quality management system. A note has been added to allow organizations the flexibility to select common sense, value-added metrics that relate to conformance to product requirements and the effectiveness of the quality management system.
8.2.4 – Monitoring and measurement of product	Changes were made to specify that authorization for the release of product and the actual release of product or service refers to final product/service prior to delivery to the customer.
8.5.2 – Corrective action	A change was made to indicate that multiple causes may contribute to nonconformities. Verification of corrective action was clarified. The standard now specifies that the organization must review the effectiveness of corrective actions taken.
8.5.3 – Preventive action	The standard now specifies that the organization must review the effectiveness of preventive actions as well.

About the Author

From 1991 until 2008, Ann W. Phillips was President of Quality Techniques, Inc. During that time she assisted numerous companies, ranging from small distributors to worldwide corporations, in their pursuit of ISO 9001, QS-9000, or ISO/TS 16949 registration. More than one hundred fifty clients achieved registration. A sampling of the industries and organizations with whom she has worked includes:

Manufacturing:
- Chemical
- Automotive
- Aerospace
- Pulp and Paper
- Container Corporations
- Medical Products

Services:
- Shipyards
- Engineering and Consulting Firms
- Medical and Health Services
- The Federal Aviation Administration
- Distributors
- Transportation

Her emphasis is on implementing practical and effective management systems in a way that achieves measurable improvements in the business. Ms. Phillips is certified by the Registrar Accreditation Board as a Quality Systems Auditor.

Prior to August 1991, Ms. Phillips worked with 3M and Dupont as a Quality Engineer, Quality Manager, and Occupational Health and Safety Supervisor. During that time, she audited quality management systems at numerous supplier organizations; lead the ISO 9001 implementation process at a chemical facility; and coordinated safety and health systems with the ISO 9001 management system.

In addition to on-site consulting and training, Ms. Phillips has instructed regularly for the University of Houston at Clear Lake, the Center for Quality at Eastern Michigan University, Collin County Community College, the American Society for Quality (ASQ), and the American Production and Inventory Control Society (APICS). She participated on a small task force to write the US supplement to ISO 19011. She is a popular speaker at management system conferences throughout the country.

Index

Page numbers in *italics* refer to tables or illustrations.